Women
and Shares
in Australia

Women and Shares in Australia

How to start buying shares and secure your financial future

Robyn Murtagh

The Five Mile Press

TO MY AUNT AND COUSIN

The Five Mile Press

The Five Mile Press Pty Ltd
22 Summit Road
Noble Park Victoriia 3174
Australia

Published in 2000
Reprinted 2001

This book is copyright. Apart from fair dealing for the purpose of private study, research, criticism or review, as permitted under the Copyright Act, no part may be reproduced by any process without the written permission of the publisher.

Text copyright © Robyn Murtagh 2000
Cartoons copyright © Lisa Coutts 2000

Editor: Maggie Pinkney
Designer: Lucy Adams

Printed in China

National Library of Australia
Cataloguing-in-Publication data

Murtagh, Robyn
Women and shares in Australia: how to start buying shares and secure your financial future.

Includes index
ISBN 1 86503 396 0.
1. Stocks – Australia. 2. Women – Australia – Finance, Personal. 3. Investments – Australia. 4. Stock exchanges – Australia. I. Title.

332.6322

COVER PHOTOGRAPH: Courtesy Photodisc Australia Pty Ltd

ABOUT THE AUTHOR

Robyn Murtagh holds a Bachelor of Laws from Melbourne University, and was admitted as a barrister and solicitor of the Supreme Court of Victoria. After practising law for some years she went to London where she worked in the human resources department of a large multinational company. On her return to Australia she continued working in this field, and completed a major in psychology at Melbourne University.

During the eighties she was trustee of a large superannuation fund. This was the beginning of what was to become a lifetime interest in the sharemarket. Since 1992 she has divided her time between running a farm, breeding thoroughbred racehorses and actively investing and trading shares on the stockmarket.

In 1995, after completing a Master of Taxation at Melbourne University, Robyn began teaching part-time at the Council of Adult Education, Melbourne, where she designed a course specifically aimed at educating women in the area of direct share ownership. Currently, she teaches courses for both beginners and more experienced sharemarket investors.

ACKNOWLEDGEMENTS

I would like to thank the people who have assisted and encouraged me in writing this book. These include:

Sharron Dickman for her advice and help, Janet Day for her understanding and endless proofreading, Neil Day, who always managed to fix my computer, Sandra Welsman for constantly pushing me to write and, most of all, my editor Maggie Pinkney, who suggested this project in the first place – and has helped me every step of the way. And a special thank you to Gerry Pauley for his wit, wisdom and support. I would also like to thank John Dunton and Carmel Di Mattia of the CAE and all the women who have participated in my courses. They have been both a joy and inspiration to me for many years. My beloved aunt and cousin have been a mainstay during this project, but I will leave them their anonymity, as I will those friends whose biographical details have helped enliven and humanise this book.

CONTENTS

Introduction   9

1   What's the Best Way to Invest Your Money?   17

2   Getting Down to Basics   25

3   Learning to Love the Stock Exchange   40

4   A Taxing Chapter   51

5   Other Ways of Investing in the Market   63

6   Who's the Right Broker for You?   75

7   What Makes the Market Rise or Fall?   87

8   Getting Started on Your Portfolio   98

9   Building Your Portfolio   114

10   Researching the Market   128

Frequently (and Not-so-frequently)
Asked Questions   141

Afterword   147

Index   151

'From birth to eighteen a girl needs good parents. From eighteen to thirty-five she needs good looks. From thirty-five to fifty-five, a woman needs personality; and from fifty-five on the old lady needs cash.'

Kathleen Norris, 1880-1966
American novelist

INTRODUCTION

Controlling Your Finances – and Your Life!

Contact with friends – and years of interaction with women taking my stockmarket classes – have convinced me that a major gender divide exists when it comes to investing in the sharemarket. Generally, women only receive significant sums of money upon retirement, or when they are bereaved, retrenched or retire – and all these events are extremely stressful. So it's when women are at their *most vulnerable* that they turn to financial advisers for guidance.

Unfortunately, most women tend to view investment in general, and the sharemarket in particular, as complex, mysterious – and best handled by an 'expert'. This lack of self-confidence is particularly true of older women. However, my classes are also full of young women who know nothing about investment. The most frequent comment I get from this group is, 'Why weren't we taught this at school?'

Anxiety and ignorance are in turn nourished by self-interested groups who encourage women to worry about their financial futures. This 'worry' is then supposedly alleviated by encouraging these women to place their trust (and money) with advisers, fund managers or accountants who will 'take care' of them. Advertising repeatedly encourages women to leave investing in the stockmarket to those profoundly wise and experienced mortals who 'know what they are doing' (or who, in my language, know what product they are selling) and who won't panic in a downturn (perhaps!). The less women know the easier the product is to sell.

In my courses I have met many women, each with their own unique lives. This has led me to taking a holistic approach to the subject of investment. Your lifestyle and the way you support yourself financially are fundamentally intertwined. You may not agree that money makes the world go around, but unless you want to go and live in the forest with a begging bowl you'll need financial resources. Achieving financial security is something you'll need to consciously work at. It means saving and investing during your working life, and careful investing in income-earning growth assets when you are no longer working. While this involves self-discipline, it doesn't mean you must base your life on a long-term corporate plan, a daily 'to do' list and general deprivation. I have never set formal goals for myself – I'm not even good at making out a shopping list! But I've had a determination to be financially self-sufficient. My aim was to live my life without constantly having to worry about money.

To those of you who are suffering loss of self-esteem, for whatever reason, try to look at your situation positively. To be truly happy you have to be living a life that suits you, and that may be like no one else's. There is a lot of pressure on us to conform to 'normal, desirable' standards – and sometimes we feel a sense of failure because we don't. I can remember when I was a little girl being very upset because our family was not like the one on the television series *Father Knows Best*. There was no mention of the dysfunctional family then, and I felt that ours was the only family that didn't measure up to the one on television. Much later, as a divorce lawyer, I discovered that my family was not so different after all.

By the same token, we all tend to think that other people are smarter and better informed than we are (of course some are, but not as many as you think). This mistaken belief leads us to entrusting our money to people whose integrity and wisdom we believe in. Unfortunately, we are often let down, mainly because we haven't educated ourselves sufficiently to know what they are doing with our money.

From the outset, I've been profoundly influenced by my aunt, a lady of advanced years, who can't understand this idea of 'worrying' about investing your money. 'How does anyone who isn't in the stockmarket expect to make money?' she asks. My own belief is that money may not buy happiness, but financial literacy and security will certainly give you more options in life. Perhaps I underestimate the care and concern of my loved ones, but I feel considerably more secure knowing I have enough money to finance my declining years.

While this book covers the fundamentals of investing, I don't intend to go into highly technical details. I've aimed to produce a technically correct, readable guide based on my own experiences, and those of my friends – and I hope you'll be able to relate to them.

My major objective is to persuade you to put your fears aside and to take charge of your own financial future. This doesn't mean standing in front of a mirror repeating affirmations, but rather taking charge of your life in a meaningful and positive way. I don't have a quick-fix solution. It takes work, time and patience to become adept at anything – and you need to start at a very basic level.

My students often say to me, 'It's all very well for you. You know so much'. It's true that I have achieved financial independence, but it is not true that this came easily. I don't reveal this in my classes, but I started off from a pretty shaky base when I was retrenched from a job I had held for nineteen years. Sheer length of service gave me entitlement to (including superannuation) a significant termination payment.

This was comforting, but did little for my self-confidence. Effectively, I was being paid to go, to leave the tribe. The new managing director even gave me a little homily on 'not looking back'. As it happened, the way I felt I wasn't really tempted!

At around the same time I was retrenched from work, I learned that I'd also become redundant in my most important personal relationship. Not a great year! There I was – dumped, jobless, nearly fifty, vulnerable and insecure.

Apart from my termination money the only other 'asset' I had was a small horse-breeding farm run by a manager, and eating up vast amounts of money. What to do? Obviously, I had to make profound changes – and it was critical that these changes should provide a firm foundation for the rest of my life. With my social and financial underpinnings gone, I decided to take a holistic approach to my situation. My first priority was to re-establish myself mentally, emotionally and physically. Only after that could I concentrate on the financial aspects.

As part of the outplacement process my ex-employer arranged financial counselling. Here I met the first of many financial advisers all eager to look after my money. No one thought I might be able to do this myself. Rather than following my first mentor's advice and committing myself to remaining in the superannuation framework (which in my case would have been disastrous), I parked the money in a no-entry-or-exit fee rollover fund suggested by my accountant. (Moral: *always get a second opinion.*)

This gave me time to make a concerted effort to pull myself together: a process involving, among other things, yoga, meditation and contemplation (including six weeks in an ashram in India). This self-examination was very important. Until I achieved equilibrium, and stopped beating myself around the head for being so inadequate, I was incapable of rationally deciding what I'd do with the rest of my life.

It's never a good idea to make important financial decisions while you are vulnerable, yet this is often the very time when you are under the most pressure to do so. You may be facing bereavement, job loss, the breakdown of a relationship or – like me – you can hit the jackpot with a combination of catastrophes. If this happens take time out. Under no circumstances allow yourself to be rushed into hasty decisions. You can actually improve your situation if you take time to think about it clearly. Of course, decisions can't be delayed indefinitely – you need to use this time out to come to reasonable and rational conclusions.

After a painful coming to terms with most of my emotional baggage I was ready to face the future – bleak though it then looked. It was clear that my age seriously precluded me from finding another job, and I didn't fancy the idea of facing further rejection trying. As a start, I let the farm manager go and began working on the farm myself. That saved a lot of money and got me out of bed in the morning.

For a multiplicity of reasons I enrolled in a Master of Taxation degree specialising in company law. (To know something about company taxation you have to learn something about the way companies work). Being shaken by the results of an intelligence test that demoted me from the top 5 per cent to the bottom 30 per cent of the population, I needed to do something really challenging to prove to myself that I was still intellectually capable!

It was by no means smooth sailing, and at first the Masters seemed impossible to achieve. Despite having a law degree I was starting off from a limited knowledge base, and all the other participants were practising accountants or lawyers. Still, I had a few things going for me: I was prepared to work hard, I was interested in the course content and, above all, I was prepared to sound stupid.

I can't over-emphasise how important it is to forget your pride and have the courage to ask questions. Never be diffident about asking questions because you are afraid of sounding stupid. For the first year I did sound stupid, very stupid, as I struggled to come to grips with difficult technical subjects. Things improved during the next few years – partly because I knew more, and partly because everyone had got used to my questions. This was academically the hardest thing I have ever done and I was both pleased and relieved when I got the degree.

After careful consideration I decided that my financial future would best be provided for outside the superannuation framework. I also decided that investing directly in the stockmarket was my preferred course of action. Without looking at any alternative brokers, I entrusted my affairs to a stockbroker simply because he came highly recommended by somebody I considered a financial genius (the same person who told me not to look back).

This broker may have been suitable for a highly experienced investor, but for me the whole episode was a nightmare and turned out as arguably the worst financial move I have made so far. Details of this dreadful encounter appear in Chapter 6. It didn't take me long to realise that things were not as they should be, and I soon dispensed with the services of this frightful stockbroker.

After that my studies, an experienced cousin and a rising stockmarket provided the basis for my financial future. Since then I've made countless errors but none as large as trusting the wrong person with all of my money. (I have to confess I was very flattered that my stockbroker called me every day. At that time no one else did.)

From then on, investing in the stockmarket has provided me with financial independence. I have tried real estate but found myself temperamentally unsuited to it, as I go to pieces when there are tenant problems. While I breed racehorses and have a high tolerance of risk, I seldom buy speculative shares. My portfolio largely comprises quality companies, of which, in most cases, I am a proud part-owner.

I have learned many lessons, the overriding one being that – as with so much of life – you only get out what you put in. *There is nobody more concerned about caring for your money than you are, and to make meaningful decisions or to even ask meaningful questions you must be prepared to educate yourself.* I'm not suggesting you rush out and enrol for a higher degree, but I am recommending you put in the time and effort to become financially literate. This need not be an overwhelming or boring task. Money is interesting, particularly when it is yours; just look at all those other people interested in your money and it's not even theirs – not yet anyway! I want you to approach investing in the stockmarket with a positive attitude. Be prepared to work at it.

Seek financial advice but be prepared to question that advice, and under no circumstances give in to the temptation of relying on any one person.

I've found it very sad meeting women whose husbands have died suddenly, leaving them vulnerable to financial 'experts'. Recently a student of mine explained to me why she felt it a positive thing that her husband had shocked her with his infidelity. 'I was a very devoted wife who left all the decisions to "Tom". Had he suddenly died, I would have been totally unprepared and unable to cope. This way I was shattered, but I have had time to adjust and take responsibility while he is still around. It's amazing, but whatever happens I now know that I can manage both financially and emotionally.' Her husband's lifestyle makes it likely that he will go sooner rather than later and her attitude is a very sensible one. She has certainly turned a negative experience into a positive one.

Hopefully, you will never have to face the sort of shock treatment she did. However, I do feel that, in the words of the Boy Scouts, we should all *be prepared*.

Robyn Murtagh
Melbourne, 2000

1

WHAT'S THE BEST WAY TO INVEST YOUR MONEY?

In this chapter I'll help you understand the difference between various types of investment. And I'll introduce you to the concepts of growth and non-growth assets, concentrating on shares and real estate. Broadly speaking, all investments can be classified into two categories: *growth* and *non-growth*.

Growth and Non-growth Investments

Growth investments include shares and property. With these investments you are hoping not only that the income from the investment will increase but also that the capital value of your asset will grow over time. Collectables can also be counted as growth investments, but these don't generate income.

Non-growth investments comprise bank deposits and other types of fixed income where the capital value of your original investment remains the same.

Unfortunately, where there is the potential for capital growth there is also the potential for capital loss. However, it should be remembered that there is also the potential for capital loss in non-growth investments. This is best illustrated by thinking of what goods cost ten years ago, and what they cost now: *a lot more*.

Over time, the value of money declines due to inflation. *The greater the inflation the more rapidly the cost of things your money can buy rises, and the more money you need to maintain your purchasing power.* If you are living off the income of your investment, and the capital amount you have in the bank remains unchanged, your money will buy less.

When comparing investments it is important to compare like with like. It is pointless to examine a 'compounding' scenario, where you touch neither capital nor interest – and interest is then paid on the interest – if in fact you plan to live off the interest. This is why growth is so important. Your asset grows while you are living off the income (if you reinvest the income it will grow even faster). When interest rates are high, leaving your money in a bank account can be a very satisfactory way of increasing your funds. But of course high interest rates also mean high inflation rates, so you still need to have a good look at your 'real' income level.

The 'Age and Safety' Myth

I often read that the older you are the more you should invest 'safely', that is, in non-growth investments. I don't understand this view, as I feel the type of investment that is suitable for you depends on how long you can invest the money for. If you know that on a certain day you will need to retrieve an investment – for example, if you are leaving employment and have to withdraw your superannuation – then you have a defined time horizon and must protect your capital as you have no time to recover any losses.

But once you are retired, your investment has to last the rest of your life, and your time horizon dramatically extends. At this stage, you could be *looking at another thirty years, so you need an investment that will both grow and provide you with an income* for as long as is necessary. In my opinion, you shouldn't get too disheartened by the thought of using capital from time to time. If you buy the 'safe' product alternatives of annuities or pensions you are in fact receiving interest plus the return of your capital.

> ### It's OK to Spend Capital – Sometimes
> My aunt has for many years held a modest portfolio of quality stocks. Over this time she has not hesitated to sell shares when she has needed extra money. Because she has invested wisely, this has not really depleted her capital as the value of the remaining shares have been constantly rising.

Shares Are for the Long Haul

Studies have shown that over the long term, say ten years-plus, shares as a category have outperformed other asset classes. This doesn't necessarily mean you'll have to wait ten years for capital growth. (If you invested in the initial float of Telstra – as opposed to the subsequent float – you would have been in a growth/profit situation from day one.) Rather, shares are like any other asset you hold – you never willingly put yourself into a situation where you are a desperate vendor, forced into a quick sale.

> ### Wise Share-sellers Wait and Plan
> My neighbours, who were first-time share buyers, bought a large number of shares in the Tabcorp float. A few years later they came to me asking how they could sell their shares. I suggested they perhaps sell some now, some in the next financial year (to even out their capital gains liability) and that they hold on to some. But they said no, they couldn't do any of that, because they had signed a contract for house renovations and needed all the money within two weeks.
>
> The good news was that because the shares were so liquid they received their money within a week. The not-so-good news was that they had to take the prevailing price. While they made a handsome profit they lost too much in tax. And since that time, the value of these shares has risen substantially. Had they waited and planned they could have paid for the renovations and still had some shares left. (Their net proceeds would have been much higher with minimal tax planning). Unfortunately they looked on their renovations, rather than their shares, as a long-term investment.

What's Better – a Share or a House Brick?

Shares in large companies are very liquid. Any time when the market is open you can sell your shares and be confident of the exact amount you will receive. It is this constant valuation that reinforces the view that the sharemarket is volatile, particularly in comparison to the real estate market.

But think about it; you really only know with absolute certainty the value of your real estate on two occasions – the day you buy it and the day you sell it. The rest of the time you can think or dream what you like. Were real estate subject to the same ruthless public scrutiny as shares there is no doubt it would be considered more volatile than is currently the case.

> ### The Real Estate Rollercoaster
> Here's an example of how volatile real estate can sometimes be. A friend of mine bought a house for $364,000 the weekend before the property crash in 1989. Subsequently she spent a great deal of money on the house. In 1995, when it was again valued, she was confident its worth had risen. She was shocked when the value came in under $300,000.

While hopefully increasing in value and providing a tax-effective income, shares require no maintenance or repairs, are not subject to rates taxes or insurance and never have problems with defaulting or destructive tenants. I'm not saying you shouldn't invest in real estate, but I am trying to put into perspective the love affair Australians have with bricks and mortar. Needless to say, my house-buying friend (see panel above) originally bought the house because she fell in love with it. (And this is not necessarily the best state of mind to be in when making major investments.) I can say categorically that, while it's possible, it's much harder to fall in love with a company share.

If you do decided to invest in shares it's best to start off in a modest way and gradually build up your portfolio.

> ### SMALL OUTLAYS GREW TO $54,000
> Friends of mine had never invested in the stockmarket. They started off by each buying 100 National Australia Bank shares at $10.50 each (total cost $2100). Over the next five years they reinvested their dividends and twice a year topped up their holding with the bank's share purchase scheme. They now have 1000 shares each valued at $27 per share. Had I suggested initially that they spend $54,000 they would have thought I had gone mad. This way they have a savings plan and a valuable investment.

Unlike shares, property is high cost, both in terms of the amount of money you need to invest and in terms of entry and exit fees. People regularly borrow large sums of money to purchase a single unit, hoping they'll find a reliable tenant – and that the value of the unit will increase.

This is what I call an all-or-nothing investment – you can't buy or sell the odd bedroom, nor can you gradually add to your holdings.

> ### SHARE PROFITS ARE QUICKER, CHEAPER
> I recently sold a unit in the inner city, and the agent was ecstatic that he had achieved a thirty-day unconditional sale. I couldn't help reflect that when I sell shares, I have the money in a week (provided the broker is competent), have no advertising or legal fees and pay less than half the amount involved in commission.

Many Australians have their largest assets tied up in two investment categories: their house and superannuation. Unlike shares, neither of these investments is liquid. You can't readily access your super fund or your house for cash.

Not All Shares Are the Same

Not all shares are equal. As I will remind you time after time, when you buy a share you are buying part-ownership of a business. Of course, there's a huge difference between buying a share in a going enterprise like Woolworths and a speculative share in a junior miner or small pharmaceutical company that has yet to find gold or market a product. When you are starting off a portfolio most advisers would rightly recommend that you buy into proven quality companies. These are called blue-chip investments – after the highest value chips in the casino. (But I'm not too sure about the appropriateness of this name.)

Never Be a Wishful Thinker

When I ask the women in my classes what shares they have, I am often surprised to find they hold highly speculative shares. When I ask why, I am invariably told that they were given a 'tip'. Now, I race horses, but rarely punt. I feel that I am taking enough risk in merely being an owner. But I'm in a minority. People are forever asking me for racing tips. 'Stable' information, even when it isn't very good, is highly prized. It seems everyone thinks there is a mystical insider track to riches. Well sometimes – very occasionally – there is, but most of the time the whole thing is wishful thinking. Indeed, if you try to give a realistic assessment of your horse's chances you are invariably cut off with a 'Just tell me if it is going to win'. And so it is with shares: 'Just tell me it's going to go up' is as much as most people want to hear.

Someone to Watch Over You? It Isn't Necessary!

Deep down, most of us want to rely on someone else, someone who cares about us and is preferably the fount of all knowledge. There is a popular song called 'Someone To Watch Over Me', and one of the lines goes 'I never wanted diamonds or pearls – just one who'll watch over me', and despite changing social attitudes I get the strong feeling that this still applies. Well, with this attitude you certainly won't have to worry about being inundated with diamonds and pearls.

When You Buy a Share You Buy Part of a Company

Because owning a share is owning part of a company, it is a good idea to find out something about the business which you're investing in before you become a part owner, rather than relying solely on someone else's information. This doesn't necessarily have to be a highly technical exercise. For example, we all shop. Which store would you like to be a part owner of? I will discuss in some depth how to find out about companies in Chapter 10.

INVEST ETHICALLY – AND SLEEP AT NIGHT

When I was first investing I bought shares in what I thought was a stockfeed and salt company. I soon discovered they were also owners of several intensive piggeries, a practice I abhor. I should have looked at everything they did before I invested.

The Greater the Risk the Greater the Return

You should also keep in mind the much-vaunted maxim that risk equals reward – and vice versa. If a company is offering a much greater return than its peers look carefully before investing. Pyramid Building Society advertised higher rates than its competitors. Why? Because it was making riskier loans and charging higher interest rates. When its debtors could not pay, the whole structure collapsed.

Keep Your Head in a Crisis

To reiterate, when you invest in a share you are becoming the part-owner of a company. While your share of the business can be sold quickly, essentially you are buying a long-term investment. As a conservative investor you should be anticipating steady rather than spectacular growth. There will be times when your share of the business is more highly valued by the market than others, but at all times you must keep your head, and remember your long-term vision. I'll discuss later when you should sell. But always have a good reason, other than simply that the market has dropped. In 1987 many investors sold out cheaply only to have to re-buy at much higher prices when the market recovered. I'm not talking here of the companies run by the entrepreneurs who financed their own lifestyles at the expense of other shareholders, but of well-run companies whose share prices dropped in sympathy with the general market.

Collectables – the High-risk Investment

I'm not going to cover collectables here. Firstly, they produce no income; secondly they require expert knowledge; thirdly, accidental damage can destroy their value and, finally, they are certainly not liquid. They are in fact high risk, often without the high reward. If you want to collect as a hobby, fine. If your collection increases in value, that's good. But unless it's your business *don't confuse a lifestyle decision with financial investment.*

2

GETTING DOWN TO BASICS

No matter what you do, whether it's cooking or sailing, you need to learn a few basic principles and technical terms. So it is with the stockmarket. These terms will seem strange at first, but provided you know what they mean, they will soon become useful. You'll pretty soon discover that, unless you grasp the basic terms, later discussions about the stockmarket become meaningless.

In Chapter 1, I emphasised that when you invest in a share you are buying a small part of a business or a *limited liability company*, 'listed' on the stock exchange.

The advantage of investing in a limited liability company is that, unlike a partnership, your liability is limited to the fully paid value of the shares. *Once you hold fully paid shares there is no further liability.*

Why Does a Business List on the Stockmarket?

As a business grows it needs more capital and its owners may seek to raise funds by offering shares in the company to the public. Frequently, the owners of a company that is listing will maintain control by retaining a large slab of the company. Retaining shares demonstrates that the vendor has confidence in the company's future. Because vendor shares are held in 'escrow', and usually can't be sold for two years, the reduced number of shares on the market often leads to scarcity and an increased share price.

> ### A Cleverly Designed Float
> When Publishing and Broadasting Limited floated off ecorp they kept 80% of the business. This raised capital while PBL both retained control and benefited from any rise in ecorp's share price.

A company can only apply to the public for funds if it meets stringent legal requirements. If you wish to participate in a float you must apply for shares in the business through an application form in the *prospectus*. This ensures potential investors at least have a prospectus even if they fail to read it.

Read the Prospectus First!

The prospectus must set out full details of the company, including its expected financial performance and any risks that may hinder the company achieving its financial forecasts. Investors are then invited to apply for shares in the company in return for a share of the *future profits*. These newly created shares are offered at an issue price payable either immediately (fully paid) or by instalments (partly paid).

When you are examining a prospectus you should bear in mind that financial projections are just that. They are only as good as the underlying data they are based on. Generally, government enterprises will be more conservatively valued than private ones, as the government still has its electorate to face.

> ### Keeping the Punters Happy
> When the first parcel of Telstra shares was sold to the public it would have been political suicide for the float to be anything but a success. Therefore the government priced it so that investors would be happy. Needless to say, all the financial projections were met. As long as the government still owns part of the company it is in the interests of the vendors (the government) to keep the purchasers happy. This is particularly true if the government still owns shares it wishes to sell.

At the time of writing, the share price of Telstra 2 is below its issue price. It's interesting to note that in 1993 the government priced a second tranche (block of stock) of Commonwealth Bank shares at $9.35. The share price later sank to below $8 and remained there for nearly two years. However, currently CBA shares are worth more than $27.

On the other hand, private vendors are often seeking the maximum return for their asset, and are only inhibited by the prospect of the issue being undersubscribed – that is, if the shares are considered so expensive that purchasers are deterred from buying them.

Generally, if a company has been unprofitable in the past it is unwise to assume its profits will shoot up merely because your money is now in it. Look carefully at what the company does, and at the section setting out future risks, and make your own assessment. Don't invest merely because a well-known or respected figure features in the company.

> SAD CASE OF THE SHRINKING MILLIONS
>
> Network Entertainment, launched in November1996, raised some $12 million from the public. Dr John Hewson was its chairman. Within six months Dr Hewson had departed, and two months later the company went into liquidation.

Think Before You Buy

Do some research before you exchange your hard-earned money for shares. The financial press will usually express an independent opinion. But don't just rely on what you read and hear. Often you can use your own common sense. For example, if you notice that a certain city store is never crowded it is probably not a good idea to invest in it. And don't be over-impressed by the difficulty or otherwise in obtaining stock – it's not necessarily relevant. For example,

Victoria's Tabcorp stock was readily available and found very little favour – largely due to the uncertainty created by the then leader of the State Opposition John Brumby, who talked about reversing the privatisation when Labor was returned to power. On the other hand, Melbourne's Crown Casino was much sought after and difficult to obtain on the float.

As it turned out Tabcorp has more than quadrupled its float price, while Crown (before it was taken over by PBL) sank to a fraction of its issue price. Tabcorp proved to be an infinitely better stock.

> ### A Careless Investment Cost Thousands
> My neighbour is a very busy computer expert. One morning, while chatting over a truckload of stable manure, he asked me about a particular float. This float had been the subject of a most unfavourable report in the *Australian Financial Review*, and I offered to get the article for my neighbour. 'Oh, I wouldn't have time to read that. And besides, I've already sent the cheque,' he replied. He had had time to fill in a form and write a cheque, but no time to do even basic research into what he was investing in. On floating, the shares traded at less than the issue price and my neighbour has never broken even on the transaction.

It Can Be Tough Buying on the Primary Market

Buying shares at the time of a float is called buying on the primary market, and there is no brokerage or stamp duty payable. Popular floats are often intended to raise relatively small amounts of money, and consequently there are not enough shares to satisfy all the investors who want them. These floats are usually 'underwritten' by one or more brokers. (This means they will take up any shares that are not sold to the public).

Unless you are a client of the broker, and receive an allocation, you will rarely have much chance of obtaining shares in these floats (apart from some public floats such as Commonwealth Serum Laboratories.) On the other hand, you should be sceptical if a broker tries to 'sell' a float to you. Whatever story they push, it usually means that other investors aren't rushing into the float. And be warned: applying for shares in a float can tie up your money for a considerable period of time, so don't rely on an instant refund if your application is unsuccessful.

It May Be Easier Buying on the Secondary Market

After listing, shares are traded on the *secondary* market. While some investors buy shares in a float for long-term investment others, called *stags*, buy for immediate resale. If you fail to obtain stock in the float you can often buy near the float price while the stags are selling their holdings.

When the final tranche of the Commonwealth Bank was being sold it was very difficult to obtain stock. Just after listing, the market had a correction and the instalment receipts fell below their $6 issue price. That was definitely a time to buy, as the stock then took off and didn't look back.

Conversely, some stocks that are given a lot of hype are strong near the float and only later come back in price. When AMP floated the opening prices were as high as $37. After trading around the $20 mark they dipped to below $15, on the back of some disastrous managerial decisions.

SHARE-BUYER WAS TRIPPED BY A TIP

Another neighbour story (yes, the same neighbour): this time, he was certain that a pharmaceutical company called Amrad was going to be a great winner (he had been tipped!). To ensure he got enough stock he put in multiple applications, firmly believing he would be scaled back. He was surprised to get everything he had applied for. Unfortunately, the company has not lived up to his high expectations and has fallen well below its issue price on several occasions.

Once You Are a Shareholder

Once you, along with a great number of other shareholders, part own the company you're proportionally entitled to its net profits or earnings. How much of these earnings you are actually paid, in the form of dividends, depends on the company's policy. Dividends are normally paid twice a year and vary widely between companies. Generally 'growth' companies plough most of their profits back into the business. Newscorp, controlled by Rupert Murdoch, pays very little of its earnings out in dividends (about .05%), retaining the rest for expansion. The CBA, on the other hand, pays out about 77%. It's vital that before becoming a part-owner that you check on the company's dividend policy.

Many companies operate *dividend reinvestment plans* (DRPs). This means that instead of *receiving* your dividends in cash, you apply the money toward the purchase of more shares in the company. These shares are usually issued at market price, but have the advantage of no brokerage or stamp duty. If you participate in these plans you must (for tax purposes) keep careful records of the date, the number of shares acquired, and the price. A few companies also have *share top-up plans* that enable small shareholders to increase their holdings every six months. In Chapter 1, I gave an example of friends of mine who have done this with their National Australia Bank holdings. Other companies, notably Coles Myer, have very generous *shareholder discount schemes*. Check with the company for details of any of these discounts. (In my experience, such schemes are not considered important by brokers, who are sometimes unaware of them.)

You're an Owner – Have Your Say!

Theoretically you and other small shareholders control the company via voting rights. But in reality you have very little influence over company policy. Only major shareholders with large blocks of shares can exercise real control.

However, this doesn't mean that you can't voice your feelings. Company directors must face you at annual general meetings, where you can ask whatever you like.

If you *do* want to ask a question, be prepared, be patient and, above all, don't be diverted by the smell of brewed coffee and other goodies wafting into the room. *The more difficult the meeting for directors, the better the refreshments for the shareholders.* It may be easier to write down your question in advance in case you suffer from stage fright. Companies do take the annual general meeting seriously, particularly if things are not going so well.

COMPANY'S CHRISTMAS EVE COP-OUT

A well-known organisation which was experiencing grave problems once scheduled the company's annual general meeting for Christmas Eve. Others choose increasingly remote locations when they anticipate shareholder dissatisfaction.

Remember, you can also write to the company with any concerns you may have. Any well-run company will send a considered response. The best company managers appreciate their owners taking an interest in the business.

> SHAREHOLDER QUERIES COMPANY
>
> I own shares in a property trust that owns Southbank. One evening near Christmas I was eating in a restaurant in the complex, and was shocked to discover that several of the other eateries were closed. I wrote a rather terse letter to the company asking for an explanation. I received a very full response, together with an invitation to tour the site with a senior manager. Moral: don't sit back in silence. Your complaint could make a difference.

Basic Terms that Shareholders Need to Know

Here's a simple list of basic terms that are used to describe different sorts of shares. You don't have to learn them off by heart. Just be aware of them and, when the need arises, look them up.

Ordinary shares The most common form of share is the ordinary share. The most money you can lose is what you have paid for the share. You are also entitled to dividends and any discount offers subject to the conditions set by the company. Sometimes ownership of ordinary shares will give you preference in the event of a sale of part of the company. For example, PBL shareholders were given the right to an allocation of ecorp shares when part of that business was floated by the company.

Instalment receipts These are issued with only part of their value paid, with the rest of the payment due at a later date. For example, the initial Telstra float had a first instalment of $1.90 with a further $1.45 payable some eighteen months later. Until the second instalment was payable these were listed with only the first payment included. Despite paying for only part of the share, full dividends are usually paid to the holders of these securities. You should note that *if you're holding a partly paid share you will be legally liable to pay the second instalment when it becomes due*. Either make sure you have the money or sell the share before this date.

Similar to these are *contributing or partly paid shares*. For practical purposes, the main difference is that full dividends will not be paid on these shares until the final payment has been made.

Preference shares These shares are normally entitled to a *fixed rate of dividend on the issue value of the share* (not its trading price on the secondary market), so always check the issue price. In the event of a liquidation, preference shares rank ahead of ordinary shares – but this can hardly be considered a good reason to buy. So if you or your adviser take your place in the liquidation queue into serious consideration you should invest elsewhere. While it resembles a loan, a preference share (like an ordinary share) means you are an owner rather than a creditor of the company. This has major taxation consequences, which I will discuss later. Unless they are specified as redeemable, preference shares run on forever, and are primarily designed to *provide a constant income flow*.

You'll often obtain higher tax-advantaged income from these shares than you would from a bank deposit. This is particularly important when interest rates are low. You'll also be eligible for shareholder benefits.

Converting preference shares These shares convert into ordinary shares on certain dates predetermined by the company. Conversion into ordinary shares is set at a discount to the prevailing market price for ordinary shares – for example 10%. This fixed discount formula means that the value of these preference shares doesn't move with the value of ordinary shares. As an income stock their value is determined by outside interest rates, that is, by what returns can be obtained elsewhere.

Convertible preference shares These are convertible to ordinary shares in a specified ratio on a particular date – for example, two ordinary shares for each preference share. This kind of formula means that the shares will move in line with movements in the value of ordinary shares.

Always check precisely what you are being offered before buying these securities. If you have any doubts contact the company and get them to explain it to you.

Convertible notes These are loans to the company for a specified time with a fixed rate of return. At the end of the loan period you may be able to accept a cash settlement or, more commonly, the notes convert to ordinary shares at a pre-determined ratio – for example, one for one. These have no tax advantage over other types of interest payments you may receive, but you will probably be liable for Capital Gains Tax when your 'convertible note' is redeemed and your 'share ownership' begins.

> ### A Capital Gains Tax Surprise
> When Suncorp Metway was sold by the Queensland government, convertible notes were issued – payable by instalments. After the final payment was made the notes were 'converted' to shares. At this stage the new shareholders were assessed for Capital Gains Tax, because they had disposed of a note and acquired a share. See Chapter 4 for more on Capital Gains Tax.

Market capitalisation The market capitalisation of a company is the value of each share multiplied by the number of shares on issue.

Formula:

Market capitalisation (market cap) = number of shares on issue × current market prices. This can vary considerably. If the number of shares on issue remains the same, a value of $11 per share will give you a very different market cap from when the shares are priced at $20.

This is how the Big Australian, BHP, got to be the Much Smaller Australian. Conversely, Newscorp shares went from $14 to $26 making that company the largest by market cap on the Australian Stock Exchange.

Dilution As a shareholder you are entitled to a piece of the profits in proportion to the number of shares you own. To work out your entitlement *the net profits are divided by the number of shares on issue*. This is *called earnings per share*.

Formula:

Earning per share = net profits ÷ number of shares on issue

The earnings per share are influenced by two factors: *the size of the profits and the number of shares on issue. Increasing the number of shares on issue automatically dilutes the earnings per share*. If the size of the corporate pie (profits) remains the same, the more shares there are, the smaller each individual piece will be.

Conversely, the smaller the number of shares on issue the greater the size of each individual piece. It is in this context that the following share issues should be understood.

Share splits Splitting existing shares varies the price of those shares but doesn't dilute overall earnings per share. Instead of holding one $10 share you now hold two $5 shares. Companies tend to do this when their share price is so high that investors are psychologically unprepared to buy. Conversely, shares can be consolidated without any change to overall earnings per share.

> **From $2000 a Share to $4**
>
> Transurban shares were trading at $2000 per share, making them very illiquid. A share split was carried out on the basis of 500 to 1. This had the effect of valuing each share at $4 without altering the market capitalisation or the earnings per share of the company.

Bonus shares These are a special issue of shares given to existing shareholders in proportion to their existing holdings. For example, for every 10 shares you own you are sent an additional one. However, because an additional 10% of shares has been created, unless a company can increase its earnings by 10% – and maintain its dividend – the value of the shares over time will fall by 10%. You don't pay for bonus shares and can't refuse them. But they are no longer popular with companies, and are rarely issued.

Company options An option gives the holder the right, but not the obligation, to acquire a share in the company at a specified price on a specified day. Company options are usually issued some years before expiry. *Companies issue options because they need money* or as a reward to shareholders or staff. There is usually a long period between the starting up of the business and the generation of cash flow from its products. Typical examples would be Internet technology and pharmaceutical companies. The value of an option will move up and down with the underlying share price and the amount of time to expiry. Holders are not entitled to dividends (if the main shares don't pay dividends this is not a consideration), and if the options are not exercised on the appropriate day they expire worthless. The only time you would not exercise an option is if the cost of converting to a share was greater than the worth of that share. If a large number of options is exercised on the same day the number of shares on issue is substantially increased. Sometimes options can be issued instead of shares to cement alliances with other companies.

IT Firm's Dilution Solution

The IT company MultiEmedia granted 29,206,696 options (which represented 10% of the issued capital of the company) to Computershare to be exercised at a price of 50 cents within a year of approval by company shareholders at an extraordinary general meeting. At the time of the issue MultiEmedia shares were about 72 cents. Clearly the company believed that the dilution effect would be offset by increased future earnings.

Unfortunately, at the time of writing, shares in this company have fallen below 20 cents.

Rights issues Rights issues are an offer from a company to existing shareholders to buy additional shares (on a proportional basis) at a predetermined price. This will always be less than the market price when the offer is made. There are several matters to consider when deciding whether to take up a rights issue.

The first and fundamental question is: *why are they asking for more of my money?* The company will send a prospectus with the rights issue, and you should look at this very carefully. Remember this issue will create more shares and therefore *earnings must increase* to cover the dilution.

Cash Required – for a Solid Reason

Paladin Commercial Trust had a one-for-three rights issue. The purpose of the issue was to pay for a new building in Sydney. Details of the building, the tenants, terms of leases, etc., were provided, together with estimated increases in cash flow. The project was in keeping with its general business and looked sound. This issue was fully subscribed. We all knew why they wanted our money and the share price remained substantially above the issue price.

> **WHY DID THEY WANT THE MONEY?**
>
> Healthscope had a rights issue at a $1.75. I was not a shareholder then, but subsequently bought shares when the price had sunk to 55 cents. Whatever they wanted the money for, it clearly did not add shareholder value. At the time of writing, these shares have sunk to a new low of 33 cents.

I'm always suspicious when a company wants my money 'to retire debt'. Does that mean the bank is pressing for repayment or that it has refused the company further funds?

If you decide not to take up the rights issue you should think very hard about holding any shares in the company at all. After the dilution caused by the rights issue you may find the value of your existing shares declines, if earnings per share go on a downhill slide.

If the rights issue is 'renounceable' the rights can be sold on the market, but unless there is a broker specified in the prospectus as giving you a special deal, brokerage on sale of the rights could exceed the sale proceeds. Usually the better the prospects of the rights issue, the greater the likelihood that there will be special arrangements for the sale of your entitlements.

If you do decide to take up the issue, wait till the last moment before sending your cheque. While the rights price will always be below the market at the time of issue, a correction in the market before the exercise of the rights could materially alter the position. The timeframe of a rights issue is usually about six weeks and you will not pay brokerage or stamp duty.

Placements Companies seeking additional capital will sometimes sell large blocks of additional shares to large institutions. While this is a quicker and cheaper way of raising money than a rights issue (there is no prospectus issued), it will dilute the holdings of existing shareholders.

> ### SHARES SLID – THEN SURGED BACK
> Novogen, a small pharmaceutical company, had approximately 70 million ordinary shares on issue. The company made a placement of approximately 8 million shares at what the shareholders were told was 'a near market price'. The value of Novogen shares immediately declined due to the dilution effect. In this case Novogen the made the placement to large institutions at near market price, and the share price eventually exceeded its previous levels.

Share buy-backs Normally the Corporations Law prohibits companies from buying back their own shares. However, in special circumstances and under strict regulation, a listed company may buy back up to 10% of its issued ordinary shares in a twelve-month period. These shares may then be cancelled, taking them out of the market. *This decreases the number of shares on offer and increases earnings per share.* In the 1980s companies tended to expand for the sake of it. In the 1990s companies were more discriminating and only made acquisitions as part of careful company strategy.

Buy-backs, along with special dividends, are a way of returning money to the shareholders. Coles Myer started this trend when, over a two-year period, it bought back 22% of its shares held by K-mart USA. Part of the reason for this buy-back was that 22% more Coles Myer shares on the market would have severely dented its share price. At that time (1994-1995) the share price for the buy-back was $4.55. Since then, the share price has increased dramatically.

Other large companies, such as the National Australia Bank and the Commonwealth Bank, have also had large buy-back programs. Subject to shareholder approval, a company can either buy a large parcel, as Coles Myer did, stand in the market as NAB does, or use some special arrangements as CBA did.

3

LEARNING TO LOVE THE STOCK EXCHANGE

When you buy shares in a float you are buying them directly from the company. This is called the *primary market* and there is no stamp duty or brokerage payable.

Once a company has been launched, via a float, it then sinks or swims on what is called the *secondary market*. The Australian Stock Exchange (ASX) regulates and conducts the trading of listed shares and other securities on the secondary market.

Shares can only be bought or sold on the Exchange by stockbrokers who, for a commission, can place, buy and sell orders on your behalf.

The Stock Exchange Automated Trading System (SEATS)

Much to the disgust of the media, who enjoyed filming frenzied scenes on the trading room floor, the floor was superseded by computer trading in 1987. Today, each stockbroker has a terminal, and each stock has a code – for example, Woolworths is WOW. When you place an order the broker feeds it into a central computer.

Prices on the secondary market are based on what price buyers (the bid) are prepared to pay and at what price sellers (the offer) are prepared to sell. Orders are placed in a queue, with priority being given to the highest bidder or lowest asking price. Where prices are equal, bids and offers are ranked at the time they were logged onto the computer. Before entering bids and offers, brokers are able to gauge the depth of the market by looking at the lists of buyers and sellers on their screens.

When there are more buyers than sellers it is called a *bull market* and when there are more sellers than buyers it is called a *bear market*.

To Queue or Not to Queue – It's Up to You!

You can decide to sell or buy at the current price or, depending on the way you think the market will move, you can ask to be logged onto the computer at a specified price.

Often brokers talk about selling at 'best' – that is, the best price they can achieve that day. In my experience this price always seems to occur immediately after you have hung up the phone. Since their income comes from commissions, most brokers prefer an immediate sale (at market) to one merely logged onto SEATS.

You can cancel or change an order any time before the computer makes a match, but once a match is made, *ownership of the shares changes* and the contract is legal and binding. Sometimes it's a good thing to join the queue, other times it isn't.

> ### Penny-pinching Didn't Pay
> While waiting for some shares I was selling to move up by 2 cents, the shares I was going to buy moved up 60 cents. In this case, I was penny-wise and pound-foolish – particularly since I was buying a greater number of shares than I was selling.

The greater the number of shares you are buying or selling the greater the difference that each cent makes. For example, if you are buying 500 shares, each cent is worth $5. (One cent × 500 is worth an overall $5.) On the other hand, if you are buying 10,000 shares, each cent is worth $100. Orders can be placed by telephone, facsimile or – depending on the broker – on the Internet.

Check Before You Sell

You must be very careful that you are clear about any orders you place. Before you place a sell order, check the number of shares you actually own.

Remember, if you're participating in dividend reinvestment or share top-up plans the number of shares you own will change every six months. On one occasion I failed to check and was left with a single share in a large company.

Be Specific When Buying

Always specify the number of shares you wish to buy and be clear about the price. Write down what you want and get the broker to read it back to you.

> ### BE ALERT – OR GET HURT
> My first broker suggested I buy 'some more' of a particular 'recovery' stock. I already owned 10,000 shares in this company but agreed to buy more. I assumed 'some more' meant perhaps 3000. Imagine my reaction when I found he had bought another 10,000 – doubling my holding in what was then a speculative stock.

Never simply tell the broker the amount in dollars that you want to invest on the stockmarket – but always be careful to specify the number of shares you want to buy. This can be of vital importance at times. For example, had you specified to a broker that you wanted $5000 worth of AMP shares the day the company floated you could have paid up to $35 per share. Eighteen months later, those shares were selling at under $15. Moral: be specific and be patient!

Make Sure You're Sent a Contract Note!

While brokers *may* e-mail, telephone or fax to advise the completion of an order, they must send same-day confirmation of any order executed in the form of a *contract note*.

This sets out all the details relating to the transaction, including the date of the trade, whether the shares were bought or sold, the settlement date, the company and the number of shares involved, the price per share and the total amount due including stamp duty and brokerage.

Be sure you receive a contract note, and if one doesn't come next day ring up and find out why. Contract notes must be kept as taxation records.

> ### Broker's Comedy of Errors
> What should have been a simple trade became a fiasco with a broker I was using for the first time.
>
> No contract note arrived – apparently the sale had been booked to another client. The broker failed to remit the sale proceeds to my bank account, and I received an account alleging I owed money for a non-existent trading account, as well as fines for failing to settle on time. How outrageous! To cap it off, the broker's advice was also incredibly poor!

Settlement is the trading day plus three days (T&3) which means that the broker must have the money and documentation relating to a sale or purchase when the transaction has occurred. There are severe penalties for late settlement.

Broker or Company Sponsorship – It's Your Choice

Broker Sponsorship

Most brokers will try to persuade you to become a 'sponsored' client under the CHESS system (Clearing House Electronic Sub System). This means you have a single security number, and all transactions are handled electronically through that broker. Whenever your holdings change you receive notification, much like a bank statement.

Brokers sell this system to clients on the basis of simplicity, but this is not without self-interest.

Sponsorship in effect locks you into using the broker who is the sponsor for that particular stock. Most brokers will send you sponsorship forms and, if you fail to specify otherwise, will automatically sponsor any shares you buy through them.

Different share lots may be sponsored by different brokers, but transactions can only be made through the broker currently sponsoring those particular shares. Some brokers provide inducements to become a sponsored client – for example, you will receive more research or be invited to client seminars.

Brokers are obliged to transfer holdings to another broker or company within 48 hours of receiving written instructions to do so. The brokers in the example above put my holdings into sponsorship despite my instructions that I wanted the stock to be company-sponsored. Since they got everything else wrong, I'm not sure why I was surprised.

Quite often it can take several written requests to move stock, and after that there is a delay while you are placed on the company register. During this time you have no holder number and can't sell the stock, which may or may not be a problem.

COMPANY SPONSORSHIP

The alternative to broker sponsorship is company sponsorship. This means the actual company sponsors you, and you have a different security identification number for each holding.

This allows you to use any broker to deal with the stock. *In either case you must keep your security holder numbers in a safe place.*

Brokers will often require that they have the funds available to pay for the shares before they will buy on your behalf.

A National Guarantee fund provides security for funds given to a broker for ASX transactions.

Some brokers recommend that you open a special cash management account to be used for transactions. This is another way of locking you in and becomes impossible if you change brokers or want to use more than one broker. *Only open such an account after very careful consideration.*

Shares are traded in minimum lots, depending on their price.

Price	Number of Shares
5-25 cents	2000
26-50 cents	1000
51cents-$1	500
$1-$10	100
Over $10	50

Normal SEATS trading takes place across Australia between 10 am and 4 pm Eastern Standard Time.

Trading Shares with Their Dividends

Dividends are declared twice a year. When directors declare a dividend they will also nominate the date the shares go ex-dividend. During the time between the dividend being declared, and the shares going ex-dividend, they are traded 'cum' (with) the dividend. *If you sell the shares during this period you sell the shares with the dividend. If you buy during this time you buy the shares with the dividend.*

By purchasing shares cum dividend you will immediately qualify for the dividend even though you have only just obtained the shares. This means that you can effectively receive three dividends in thirteen months. On the other hand, shares slip in value the day they go ex-dividend, and can be bought more cheaply at this time. Of course, you will have to wait a full six months before you then receive a dividend.

> ### CALM DOWN – IT'S THE CBA
> A friend of mine who had just started a self-managed super fund rang me in a panic. 'Commonwealth Bank shares have fallen by 80 cents. Has something happened to the bank?' I reassured her that the shares had gone ex-dividend that day.

How Do I Find Out about Payment of Dividends?

Every Monday the *Australian Financial Review* publishes details of all current dividends, the date that the shares go ex-dividend and when payment is due. Payment varies wildly between companies, so its is a good idea to check these details regularly.

Once you become a shareholder *you must notify the share registry office of the relevant company of any change of address*, so that you can continue to receive dividend advice. Most companies will pay your dividends directly into your bank account. This is a quick and convenient way of receiving a payment. The company will then send you a notice of payment with all the relevant details.

How the Stock Exchange Protects You

The ASX does not prosecute corporate criminals. This is done by bodies such as the Australian Securities and Investments Commission (ASIC). It does, however, monitor the conduct of businesses listed on the Exchange to ensure compliance with various rules and regulations.

Some of the most interesting listing rules designed to protect the investing public are the *continuous disclosure rules*. Companies must 'immediately notify the Exchange' of any material in their possession that is likely to affect the value of their shares.

To ensure compliance with this rule, companies whose share price suddenly moves up or down will be asked to give an explanation to the ASX.

> ### Casino's Change of Plans
> Melbourne's Crown Casino notified the government (before advising the ASX), that they did not propose to go ahead with certain buildings. A very public row erupted and Crown shares were suspended from trading till the matter was resolved. This was a telling demonstration of the ASX's power to enforce disclosure.

What Exactly is the All Ordinaries Index?

The 'All Ords' is regularly mentioned on TV news services, but many viewers haven't the faintest idea what it is. The Australian All Ordinaries Index was created on 1 January 1980 and is the main market indicator for the Australian Stock Exchange. Initially this index was 500 points and measured the capital gains and losses of the top 260 stocks listed on the Exchange. The Index is calculated continuously, and expressed as a number that allows you to quickly see in which direction the overall market is heading. For example, if the Index was at 2000 and the overall value of the shares measured rose by 10%, the Index would rise to 2200. The All Ordinaries represents almost 95% of the entire sharemarket by market capitalisation. (As I've already noted, market capitalisation is the number of shares on issue multiplied by the current share price.) It follows that when the share price is up, a company will have a greater market cap than when it is down, so market capitalisation is a moveable feast.

Apart from the major indicator there are several sub-indices, which allow investors to track particular classes of shares — for example there are retail, transport, banking and gold indices. If the All Ordinaries is up it does not automatically follow that every stock included will be up. But you can compare the performance of individual shares with the market generally both in the short and the long term. The greatest value of the All Ordinaries is as an indicator of the stockmarket's performance over a long period of time. The Australian Stock Exchange regularly reviews which companies should be included in the All Ordinaries, and from 1 April 2000 increased the number of stocks in the Index to 500. There are also indices covering the Top 20, 50, 100 and 200 companies, together with a small companies' index.

Since most institutions measure their performance against that of the All Ordinaries, its composition is of great importance to them, particularly those funds that link themselves directly to Index weightings (see Chapter 5). For the smaller investor, the All Ords is mostly a guide to what is happening in the overall market. There is, however, one important exception to this. *In the main, institutions invest in stocks covered by the major indices. Therefore if a stock is included or excluded from the Index it can have a substantial influence on its share price.* The faster a significant stock moves up or down, the faster the institutions will have to adjust their positions — and this gives a share price *momentum*. The recent changes to the composition of the All Ordinaries benefited some stocks included for the first time but damaged the price of any stock excluded from the Index.

LEARNING TO LOVE THE STOCK EXCHANGE 49

In addition to the All Ordinaries there is an *All Ordinaries Accumulation Index* which measures not only capital gains and losses, but includes dividends, rights issues and bonus shares. *This index assumes that all dividends are reinvested and all rights are taken up.* It is important that you always compare like with like, and if you are investing in a managed trust fund of any kind, *make sure that they are comparing their performance against the appropriate indicator.* I've seen a fund that compared its performance based on all dividends being reinvested with the All Ordinaries. Of course the fund performance looked very impressive. This is deceptive and will not be any sort of guide if you intend living off the income.

An Over-optimistic Prospectus

One particularly creative prospectus I saw promoted the fund on the basis of what would have been achieved had it been investing during the preceding three years!

Hindsight is a great thing.

The Rest of the World

The Australian sharemarket comprises about 1.3% of the world sharemarket. This compares with the USA, which controls 52% of the world market, followed by Japan and Britain with about 10.5% each. From this you will see why the American market is so important!

The major American indicator is the *Dow Jones*, which includes only 30 major stocks. The *Nasdaq* is the high high-technology exchange, and there are also a number of more broadly based indicators like the *Standard and Poors 500 Index*. All other countries with stockmarkets have their own indicators – for example, the *Financial Times Index* (London) and the *Nikkei Index* (Tokyo).

It's proposed that by 1 July 2001 the Australian Stock Exchange will be linked to the Singapore Stock Exchange. This will mean that buying shares listed on the Singapore Exchange will be as easy as buying shares on the Australian Exchange, and vice versa. Talks are also proceeding to link ten of the world's exchanges, including Australia. This proposal has many obstacles to overcome but, if it does occur, we'll see a truly global market and 24-hour trading. This may not be good news for smaller Australian companies, who could be overlooked as investors focus on the large liquid stocks.

4

A TAXING CHAPTER

Taxation is always complicated and sometimes boring, but for *any investment to be effective it must outperform inflation on a post-tax basis.* This is one reason why it is important that you have some idea of the taxation consequences of your investment decisions. The other reason you need to know something about taxation is the self-assessment system.

Self-assessment: Make Sure You Understand It

In the dim, dark past, when you or your accountant prepared your taxation return and sent it to the Australian Taxation Office, ATO officers would examine your return and issue an assessment. If you did not agree with *their* assessment you could appeal to a Board of Review. The thing to remember here is that it was the Commissioner's assessment and – provided there was no fraud or evasion – you were not penalised if he made a mistake. This has all changed. The assessing department has disappeared and *now you assess yourself.*

Provided your return is arithmetically correct you will usually get back exactly what you have asked for. I was telling this to a class when one of the students burst out laughing. 'My accountant has just rung me in triumph to say I got back what we asked for.' Well, it probably impresses most of his clients!

Like a lot of things in life, self-assessment is not as great as it sounds. The assessing department may be smaller but the audit department is much larger. If you are 'selected' for an audit, and you have made a mistake in assessing yourself, you will be faced with the payment of hefty penalty taxes. It's no excuse to claim ignorance or innocence. As for your accountant, take a look at the front of your return. The little sticker says it was all prepared on the basis of what you told him or her.

> ### Forgetting Can Be Costly
> A very sweet lady of advanced years explained to the rest of the class that she had inadvertently left some bank interest off her return. She was audited and was paying 25% additional penalty tax and, even worse, her past three years returns were now being audited and any discrepancies there would result in the imposition of even bigger penalties.

This is what makes it so important you have a basic idea of how the tax system works, and what is claimed in your return. You are the person who will be accountable for any errors.

When I raise this topic in my classes the only students who know about self-assessment are those poor souls who have been audited. The ATO has more power to investigate than the police, and they are very thorough. Even though most of my students use accountants, the workings of the system have never been explained to them. If you don't understand anything in your return ask your accountant to explain it to you *before* you sign it.

How Dividend Imputation Can Help You

This is a tax rule that is specific to share dividends and of great benefit to anyone who has dividend income. The best way to understand dividend imputation is to keep firmly fixed in your mind that *you are a part owner of the company that pays you dividends*.

Before the introduction of these rules in 1987, you paid tax twice. Firstly the company paid tax on its earnings at the company tax rate (34% at the time of writing, but due to drop to 30% in the fiscal year 2001-02). Then, after you received the dividend, you paid tax a second time at your marginal rate. In other words, you

A TAXING CHAP[TER]

were taxed twice on the same profits – when made, and then again when they were distribute the unfairness of double taxation and to enco investment that dividend imputation was introduced.

What Is Dividend Imputation?

Dividend imputation is a tax rule that enables shareholders to claim a tax rebate on dividends on which Australian Company Tax has been paid.

How Does It Work?

The tax that a company has already paid is subsequently 'imputed' to the shareholder by way of *franking credits*. This franking credit is treated as assessable income and is added to the actual cash dividend you receive.

Franking credits are provided as a *tax rebate* (deductible from the amount of tax you owe), not as a deduction (deducted against the income you make). Hopefully, the following example will help you see the way it works.

Imputation Example

Company profit $100
Company tax $34
Dividend $66

Taxpayer Marginal Rates	20% $	34% $	47% $
Dividend received	66	66	66
Plus imputation credit	34	34	34
Grossed up franked dividends	100	100	100
Tax assessed	20	34	47
Tax credit	34	34	34
Tax payable	0	13	
Credit against other income	14		

In the above example, the 20% marginal taxpayer has excess tax credits of $14. These can be used to offset tax payable on other income.

The 34% taxpayer pays no tax on the dividend. The 47% taxpayer pays $13.

You can see from this example why franking credits are particularly valuable to superannuation funds which pay 15% tax on their investment portfolio, and in turn why these funds are likely to invest in companies that pay fully franked dividends.

The Medicare Levy

Franking credits can't be used to offset the Medicare levy. This levy is paid on the entire grossed up amount (in the example on $100). This means that the levy is higher on franked dividends than on unfranked ones (dividends without tax credits).

Other Franking Credit Rules

- Franking credits not used in the financial year in which they are paid can't be carried forward to the next year but are refunded in cash.
- If you earn a total dividend income of *more than $2000 per year*, to claim the rebate you must *hold the shares for a period of 45 days* around the time that the dividend has been declared. (This rule is not designed to trap small investors but to stop large investors trading in franking credits.)
- Provided companies have franking credits to distribute, they must fully frank their dividends and distribute them equally to all holders of the same class of shares.
- *You can't choose whether or not you receive franked dividends, only whether you invest in companies that pay franked dividends.*

Why Aren't All Dividends Franked?

Remember, companies can only pay franked dividends if they have paid Australian Company Tax. Those companies with large offshore operations may not be able to fully frank their dividends. It's a quirk of the tax system that this rule effectively discourages Australian companies from operating offshore as most investors want franked dividends and punish the share price of companies that can't provide them. This is not good for our balance of payments deficit, as these companies are sending money back to Australia rather than taking it out. Other possible reasons why companies may not pay fully franked dividends are that they may be carrying forward large tax losses (plenty were in this boat after the crash of 1987), or have large depreciation allowances. These companies may only be able to partially frank their dividends.

How Do I Know if a Dividend is Franked?

If you look in the *Financial Review* on a Monday under 'Dividends Declared', you'll see some companies have an F after them. This means they are fully franked, while if companies have an F with a percentage, e.g., F55%, it means that 55% of the dividend is franked. Alternately, it can state the actual portion of the dividend that is franked, expressed in cents. When a company pays a dividend the advice to shareholders will set out the amount of the dividend, whether it is franked, and the extent to which it is franked.

Unfranked dividends are taxable at a shareholder's marginal rate.

Taxing the Tree – as Well as the Fruit

So far we have only looked at tax on dividends which are classified as income.

The most commonly used analogy for understanding the difference between income and capital is to think of a tree. The fruit is the income and the tree is the capital.

Until the evening of 19 September 1985, Australia had no Capital Gains Tax (CGT). This meant that if, for example, you bought a property and later resold it for a profit this profit wasn't taxable. No tax on capital gains led to rorting of the tax system as tax minimisation promoters found ever more exotic ways to turn income into capital and avoid payment of tax. Of course, this did not help wage and salary earners, who had no such opportunities and paid full taxation on their earnings.

All this changed when the treasurer announced the *introduction of a Capital Gains Tax effective from 20 September 1985. This tax is not retrospective, so assets acquired before that date are exempt from CGT.*

Because the tax applies to assets acquired after this date, initially not many people were affected (as most assets would have been acquired before that date). But the further we move from that date the more this tax affects us. It was because very few people were affected – at first – that the government was able to introduce draconian tax rates with very little public outcry. At that time other rules also softened the impact of the tax on low-income earners.

Acquisition of the Asset – Cost Base

On acquisition each asset has a cost base. This includes the amount you pay for the asset, plus any incidental costs incurred in acquiring it. In the case of shares these costs include the cost of brokerage, GST and stamp duty. Unless you are a share trader these costs are treated as capital and are not deductible for income tax purposes. Instead they form part of your cost base for CGT purposes.

Disposal of the Asset

The tax is triggered by the *disposal* of the asset. You should take careful note of the word disposal. *It includes sale, gift and compulsory acquisition.* The Act is very wide-ranging and, unless there is a specific exemption, CGT will apply.

> **BEWARE THIS CGT TRAP!**
> A well-known radio personality frequently advised callers to his program to transfer shares into the name of the lowest tax-paying spouse. While he pointed out that this would not incur stamp duty, he completely overlooked the CGT implications. Transfer to a spouse or other family member is a disposal for CGT purposes.

You will be liable to pay CGT when the price you receive (the consideration) less expenses is greater than the cost of the asset plus expenses. If the consideration you receive falls between the indexed cost base and the original cost base, there is no gain or loss for CGT purposes.

Where shares or other assets are gifted away *a market value will be deemed to apply* and CGT calculated on this basis.

Takeovers

Changing the nature of a pre-1985 asset may bring it within the scope of the CGT legislation. Until recently if you had shares in one company and they were exchanged for shares in a different company (as in a takeover), CGT applied.

> **A TALE OF TWO BANKS**
> When Westpac took over The Bank of Melbourne, shareholders had the option of receiving shares in Westpac. This was treated as a disposal of Bank of Melbourne shares and the acquisition of Westpac shares, so CGT applied.
>
> (No, the Commissioner didn't care that you didn't want to sell your Bank of Melbourne shares in the first place.)

In the above example, if both money and shares are received, the consideration is the combined value of the money and the shares you receive. These rules were unfair, not just because you had no choice about disposing of the shares, but because you didn't actually receive any of the money on which you were required to pay tax.

At the time of writing, the government is preparing amending legislation to grant 'roll-over relief'. Under the new law, you won't be liable to pay tax until you have actually disposed of the shares and received the proceeds. This is likely to stimulate more takeover activity involving the offer of the acquiring company's shares (scrip transfers) rather than money payment. This is easier for the acquiring company, and shareholders are no longer penalised by having to pay an unrealised Capital Gains Tax.

Remember, however, that if the nature of the asset totally changes – for example if a convertible note becomes a share, then CGT will apply.

Think very carefully before you dispose of pre-1985 assets. Always remember they are not subject to CGT gains or losses.

'FREE' TAX ADVICE PROVED EXPENSIVE

The Australian subsidiary of BTR, Nylex, was taken over by the parent company. Shareholders were offered two alternatives. They could accept a cash payment or alternatively they could take up shares in the parent company. A caller who said he bought his shares in 1985 asked a radio personality what he should do. Clearly the caller should have been asked *when* in 1985 he bought the shares. If they were pre-20 September a cash payment would be tax-free. Taking up the new shares would on disposal incur CGT liability. The question was not asked and the caller was advised to do a bit of each. It's not always a good idea to take tax advice on talkback radio!

How Special Circumstances Affect CGT

DEATH

In the ordinary sense of the word death is the ultimate disposal. *However under the Act an asset is deemed not to be disposed of as a result of death.* This is because when someone dies the first legal process is for the executor of the will to acquire the assets and then distribute the estate to the beneficiaries. If it were not for this section you could have two disposals – the first from the testator (the deceased) to the executor and the second from the executor to the beneficiary. CGT applies when the asset is disposed of either by the executor or the beneficiary. The cost base is determined by when the asset was acquired. If the asset was acquired before 20 September 1985, it is deemed to have been acquired at its market value at the date of the testator's death. This may or may not be helpful for the beneficiary. If the value of the assets is high when the testator dies, and subsequently falls, no CGT will be payable on disposal. Conversely, if the value of the asset rises (after the date of death), then CGT will be payable.

An asset acquired post-20 September 1985 is deemed to have been acquired at its actual cost, or if the testator held it for more than 12 months, at the beneficiary's or the estate's taxation rate – depending on whether the executor or the beneficiary disposes of the asset.

MATRIMONIAL SETTLEMENTS

Special 'roll-over' relief is given to assets that are transferred as a result of a Family Court decision, or as a result of an agreement sanctioned by the court. As part of this relief assets are deemed not to have been disposed of, and pre-CGT assets retain their exempt status. If you have the misfortune to wind up in the Family Court always aim for the pre-CGT assets.

Special Rules

Bonus shares distributed on shares acquired pre-20 September 1985 are exempt from CGT. Where bonus shares are distributed on shares acquired after 20 September 1985, the cost of each of the bonus shares is worked out by spreading the cost of the original shares over the original shares and the bonus shares. That is, if you originally buy 100 shares for $100 you would have a cost base of $1 per share. A one-for-10 bonus issue would give you 110 shares still acquired for $100. Your cost base would be $100 divided by 110 (your cost base per share being 90 cents). *When you have paid for shares acquired under a dividend reinvestment or share purchase plan, the amount you paid is the cost base.* Since each lot you acquire will be at a different price you must be very careful to keep precise records of the quantity date and purchase price of these shares.

Payment of CGT

Capital gains and capital losses that accrue during a year of income are netted to determine whether you have a net capital gain or loss for the year. If this results in a *capital gain it is added to your assessable income.*

If a net capital loss is incurred, it is not deductible from your assessable income, but is carried forward to be deducted against future capital gains. This capital loss is extinguished by death.

CGT SOURED A LEGACY

Laura was left a large portfolio of shares by her mother. Over the years her mother had retained her better shares and sold her loss-making ones. On her mother's death Laura was faced with either holding the shares indefinitely or paying a large CGT bill. Because Laura's mother had already sold her loss-making shares, Laura could not offset gains with the capital losses accrued by her mother. Moral: plan your finances to minimise the CGT's impact, not only on yourself but on your heirs.

If you have a low income, but the gains are still taxable, you may consider selling some shares at the end of one financial year and the rest at the beginning of the next fiscal year. The problem with this approach is that you can't guarantee what the share price will be at the beginning of the new tax year, so what you gain in tax you may lose on price. In the case of highly speculative stock, it may pay to sell when the price is high, even if you do have to pay some tax.

How is Capital Gains Tax Calculated?

For assets acquired before 21 September 1999 and, held for at least a year, a choice exists. You can either pay full marginal rates of tax on the real gain to that date (that is, on the nominal gain less the rate of inflation as determined by the Consumer Price Index frozen as from 30 September 1999), or you can pay tax at your marginal rate on 50% of the full gain.

You should ask your accountant to calculate which of the two scenarios is the most tax effective for you to use. For assets acquired after 21 September an individual pays tax on 50% of the gain at their marginal rate. Superannuation funds pay tax on two-thirds of the gain at their current tax rate of 15%. Companies pay Capital Gains Tax in full at the company rate (but remember this is declining to 30% in the year 2001-02).

Assets acquired by family trusts before 21 September 1999 will treated on the same basis as individuals. Assets acquired by family trusts after 23 December 1999 and disposed of before 1 July 2001 will also be taxed on the same basis as individuals. Assets acquired by family trusts after 23 December 1999 and disposed of after 30 June 2001 will be subject to company taxation rates on the full gain. *Gains on assets held for less than a year will be treated as income and subject to full taxation.*

When I talk about real and nominal gains, all I mean is that a real gain occurs when your investment exceeds the rate of inflation. There is no gain if your investment simply equals inflation, and if it falls short your 'gains' are illusory. As I mentioned when talking about growth assets, money left long term in the bank will usually buy less when you take it out than when you put it in. This is an example of capital being eroded by inflation.

A successful investment must outperform inflation on a post-tax basis, *but tax, while important, should never be the sole driver of any investment decision.*

Medicare

The Medicare levy is payable on 100% of net capital gains.

Franking Credits

If you have excess franking credits, you can use these to pay the tax due on capital gains (but not, of course, the Medicare levy).

...And Finally, the Much-Publicised GST

This is a most complicated tax. *The Goods and Services Tax doesn't apply to the value of shares. However it will be incorporated in fees charged for brokerage, stamp duty and services provided by financial advisers, accountants and solicitors.* If you are registered for GST you will be able to claim this component in your business activity statement. However if you are not registered (and I assume most of you are not) you claim these as tax deductions. You can claim the items in full, either on a revenue basis, where income tax applies, or as part of your capital cost where CGT is payable.

5

OTHER WAYS OF INVESTING IN THE MARKET

If you don't feel confident about investing in the sharemarket directly you may consider using a managed fund or listed investment company. Certainly, this is what your financial adviser will recommend.

Managed Funds

Managed funds are made up of individual investors' pooled money. These professionally managed funds are classified as collective investment vehicles and are set up under a trust fund structure, in which you buy units that have an entry and an exit price.

Managed funds include superannuation and other funds which cover a wide range of investment alternatives – from cash management trusts through to international equity funds.

Some funds are described as 'balanced', which means that while aiming for growth the fund holds a variety of investment classes – for example cash, property and shares. Capital guaranteed funds are not growth oriented. But they protect your capital and invest largely in fixed interest securities.

'Equity' funds will only hold shares, and these may be both Australian and overseas. Alternatively, there are some that invest in specific overseas areas, such as Asia.

Why Should I Invest in a Managed Fund?

For some people, a managed fund can mean relative peace of mind. You can start with a small sum of money and add to it on a regular basis. Your money will be spread over a range of diversified assets, making investing less risky. You can choose the level of risk you are prepared to accept, depending on your temperament and personal circumstances. The fund will be managed by experts, saving you time and, hopefully, worry. The net returns from such funds *should* exceed those that you could achieve as a private investor.

Best of all (from your adviser's point of view), the commissions received from placing your money with a particular fund should put his/her children through school. This is my fundamental problem with managed funds. *They are financial products marketed through financial advisers and accountants who have a vested interest in selling them to you.* Financial advisers usually receive a substantial *'entry' commission* when you invest, and *a yearly 'trailing' commission* to ensure you stay invested.

> ### LOOK HARD AT ADVISER'S COMMISSIONS
> Jane invested in two superannuation funds recommended by her accountant. She decided to withdraw from both funds and set up her own superannuation fund. It took two months and a great deal of argument with her accountant to leave the first fund. Withdrawing from the second fund took two weeks. ('I don't recommend that fund any more,' the accountant explained.) What a difference a trailing commission makes!

Don't think that your adviser is being scrupulously honest when he or she reveals these commissions. The law requires disclosure of any financial advantage received from recommendations. This disclosure should be in writing and expressed both as a percentage and in dollar terms. (Three per cent per annum may not sound like much, but on a $50,000 investment $1500 per annum is substantial.) It means that *before* you receive your return the fund has to pay both the fund manger and your financial adviser. There are fundamentally two different kinds of managed funds.

The Active Fund

These funds operate on the premise that they can add value to your portfolio by their asset allocation and stock-picking. The prospectus will contain glowing testimonials to successful investment teams backed up by sophisticated processes used to select stock. Fair enough – none of the funds are going to advertise that they pick stocks by throwing darts at the stock quotation pages of the *Financial Review* (though in some contests this has been the winning method). *However, never be over-impressed by slick methodology. No fund is infallible.*

> **EVEN THE BIGGEST FUNDS CAN MAKE MISTAKES**
>
> A couple of years ago my cousin, a trustee for a large super fund, showed me a fund report. The stock selection was sophisticated and rigorous. Impressed, I flipped to the stocks they actually held. I asked my cousin how, with this selection criterion, they had Newcrest, a gold miner, in their portfolio. At that time, Newcrest's share price had been devastated by an ill-advised attack on Normandy Mining, and by the fact that its biggest mine had been closed due to flooding. My cousin said he had asked this question too, and been told it had 'slipped through'.

Usually these managed funds compare their performance with one of the All Ordinaries Indices, or less often with a 'basket of commonly held stocks'. Since they get to pick the contents of the basket, it is hardly surprising that the funds always come off (theoretically) ahead. A problem with large funds is that they make very large purchases and sales, which can influence the market to the extent that they can actually make the market. It's not surprising that about 85% of funds fail to beat the Index. The most important yardstick to most fund managers is how well they are performing compared to other funds. This yardstick may not be so important to you. What is important to you is your actual financial position.

Always make sure that you are comparing a fund's performance to the appropriate index. If the fund is measuring its performance with all dividends reinvested, check that it is comparing itself with the All Ordinaries Accumulation Index. This will always be higher than the All Ordinaries, which only measures capital gains and losses. You may find that in good times the short-term performance of the fund tends to be emphasised, but when things are less rosy you are directed to look at the long-to-much-longer term, depending on how bad the present looks.

Keep in mind that a fund that has performed well during a rising market will not necessarily star in a falling market and vice versa. Remember also that you have no way of knowing whether the team who made for a successful past is still there. This is a very mobile industry and outstanding performers may either be poached by a rival fund or leave to set up their own funds. Currently, trustees of large funds engage consultants who advise them of staff movements within the industry.

While a lot of funds hug the Index some funds take a view that is different to that currently being taken by the market in general. For example, a fund may choose to hold unfashionable stocks in the belief that these provide better value than the current 'market darlings'. While these funds will under-perform in the short term, the value of these stocks is expected to increase over the medium term, and out-perform the market.

Still, it is a brave fund manager who resists buying shares when a company has market momentum and the highest market capitalisation on the ASX. Sometimes if a fund believes the market is overheated and about to correct it will move to a cash-weighted position. This is great if the market does correct, but has a terrible effect on the fund's performance if the market keeps steaming ahead. Always try to find out what your fund is doing and why.

The Index or Passive Fund

Because of the difficulty of beating the Index, and the great expense involved in trying, another sort of fund is now being promoted. These index or passive funds use computer programs to track the Index. They are aiming to replicate, not out-perform, the Index with their portfolio.

This is much cheaper but even so there are costs, and it is not really tracking the Index if the return is reduced by administrative costs and commissions. Now that we have such a multiplicity of indices you should also find out which one they are actually tracking – for example, the top 200 or 300?

Bear in mind that these funds will be moving with market momentum, and if the market suddenly changes direction on a major stock it's not going to look too good. (But then, neither is the All Ords.)

An important global index fund is the Morgan Stanley International Index (MSCI). Inclusion (or exclusion) in this fund has a profound effect on the share price of the company concerned. The CBA was included this year and consequently its share price jumped as fund-managers, replicating this index, bought the shares.

Always remember that index managers are only concerned with replicating the Index, not beating it. This means they aren't overly concerned about what they actually pay for the stock.

Underlying Assets: Something to Think About

Funds, like everything else, are only as good as their underlying assets. If the assets comprise quality Australian shares it may well be cheaper for you to hold these directly. Diversity within a share portfolio may protect you against individual calamity, but it will also mean more poor performers in the portfolio.

Reading the guidelines of the managers of one large superannuation fund, I observed that they had a policy of 'never having more than 10% invested in any one individual stock'. The portfolio contained a number of stocks including National Australia Bank whose share price had risen dramatically over a short period. I asked one of the trustees if this meant that each time NAB rose the fund sold more to keep below the 10% cap. 'Well,' he replied, 'either that, or they buy more dogs to balance things up.' When you think about it, a rule like that certainly puts a curb on the maxim of letting your profits run.

> ### BLIND LUCK SAVED A SUPER FUND
> In 1987 I was a trustee of a large superannuation fund. We had not been overly impressed by the performance of our fund manager and decided to change funds. We had six presentations made to us by the then leading fund managers. This occurred in August 1987. In hindsight it is astounding that not one of the managers who made these presentations voiced any concerns about the underlying debt problems of some of the large companies in their portfolios. Just as surprising – if they were expecting a crash they failed to mention it to us. As luck would have it we came out very well. We decided to change funds and liquidated our portfolio in Australia and overseas. We finished converting to cash one day before the crash, with no time to reinvest the money in any of the funds. By blind luck we locked in all our gains.

Overseas Funds: Be Aware of the Risks

While it is possible – particularly using the Internet – to invest directly, managed funds are generally the best way to gain exposure to overseas sharemarkets. When looking overseas you have to consider not only the company but the general economic outlook for the country and its sharemarket as well. You should appreciate that higher rewards equate with higher risks – one of the major risks being that the currency may turn against you. While funds can protect against this, insurance is very expensive and will eat into the returns.

If you are investing overseas, try to educate yourself about which countries you want to invest in – countries like South America or the Asian Tigers can be very volatile. Bear in mind that investing overseas when the Australian dollar is low can be very expensive.

Add up the Fees and Charges

Be sure to examine in detail the fees that a fund wants to charge you – and remember that *these fees come out of your money*. Ask about *fees to enter, ongoing fees and any exit fees*. Ask how and when are these calculated. Find out when and how the units in the fund are valued. Due to their multi-layered structure, Master Trusts – while convenient – are particularly expensive. You can pay up to 4% entry fees and 3% per annum. These fees may not sound high, but work out how much this is in money terms. Then work out how much the fund has to make before you see the results.

Remember, you are buying a product and products cost money. *Managers get paid for trying to beat the market whether they actually do so or not*. On one occasion when, as a trustee, I complained about a negative return, the fund manager indignantly replied, 'We didn't *mean* to lose your money.' What a relief that was!

Don't Believe All You Hear

Always remember that funds recruit clients through financial advisers. And where any commission is payable, *the adviser has a vested interest in the decisions you are making with your money.* Always be sceptical.

Recently I heard one radio 'adviser' tell a listener that, in his experience, managed funds always out-performed individual share portfolios. The information that this adviser based his views on must have been obtained from his clients, who were presumably seeing him because they were concerned about their portfolios. *What he hadn't taken into account was that private investors who were satisfied with their investments would be unlikely to seek his advice.* The sample he saw would therefore be significantly biased. Sweeping anecdotal generalisations should be treated as just that.

Something that narks financial advisers considerably is that some of the stocks that have massively out-performed the Index over the last ten years have been those floated off by the government.

If you bought into CBA, CSL, Telstra and Tabcorp at float prices your portfolio would be in much better shape than those of most of the funds. One large fund manager advertises on the basis that 'mum and dad' investors (a nice put-down) have a limited spread of stocks and are more likely to panic in a downturn and sell at the wrong time.

Without exception, it is the funds who are the first to dump stocks, often on the basis of rumour. Later they often later buy back the same stock at a higher price. The funds always receive market information before the 'mums and dads'.

> ### They Couldn't Blame the Mums and Dads This Time
> The day that Philip Bowman abruptly left Coles Myer the stock plunged to below $4. It was certainly not the 500-share discount card-holders selling out. Since then the stock has significantly increased in value.

Retirement Products: Think Before You Sign!

To coincide with government retirement polices, annuities and allocated pensions are being recommended by a number of advisers. What this means is that you convert a lump sum payment into an income stream. Deciding on this alternative is a very complex and significant decision.

Try to get genuinely independent advice before taking such a step; understand exactly why the proposal is being made. Don't make a decision based solely on perceived taxation advantages – today's tax advantage could be abolished tomorrow.

Annuities

When you buy an annuity from a financial institution you're guaranteed an agreed sum of money for a specified period of time. You receive regular payments which are made up of a return of your capital, together with interest. The interest component is subject to tax while the return of capital is tax-free.

Provided you buy your annuity from the proceeds of an Eligible Termination Payment you will be eligible for a tax rebate on the income component. There is no rebate if the annuity is purchased with other moneys.

Before you decide on an annuity you should read the proposal very carefully. *Remember, your capital is being consumed.*

The perceived advantage of an annuity is that it provides certainty of income over a period of time. But you pay for this security. You must check what happens if you wish to (or have to) terminate the arrangements. How much of your capital will be returned?

Allocated Pensions

For practical purposes these are similar to annuities, but you're only allowed to buy one using money from an Eligible Termination payment. *Each year you draw down varying amounts chosen by you within specified minimum and maximum limits.* Obviously the more you draw down, the less you'll have left.

There are significant taxation advantages currently available that are designed to push people into this income stream. However, the great tax advantages should be weighed against the fact that the poorer the fund performance, the more of your capital you'll be using. If, for example, you are 55 it's possible that you may have used all your capital by the time you are 75.

> **A Capital Miscalculation**
>
> I recently heard a talkback caller singing the praises of allocated pensions. Among other things, he pointed out that you don't have to erode your capital if, after receiving it as an allocated pension, you don't spend it. I suspect that this happy alternative would apply only to a small minority of retired people.

Where a significant sum of money is involved, and there are compelling reasons for selecting an allocated pension, you should consider the option of setting up your own allocated pension plan. This means you remain in control of your own assets.

You can select the fund categories from which the allocated pension is drawn but if, for example, you choose a capital stable fund (which is largely made up of fixed interest securities), you should compare the costs of investing through your own fund versus the costs you pay in a capital stable or capital-guaranteed fund.

It's not difficult to set up your own fixed interest investments.

CGT Can Rub Salt in Your Wounds

Managed funds make profits in different ways. Share dividends will mostly be fully franked. Capital gains from buying and selling shares will not. Unlike companies, these kinds of trusts don't pay tax.

Instead, all profits and tax credits are distributed to the unit holders or beneficiaries who are then taxed at their marginal rates. *Where the capital gains exceed the franking credits, you will be required to pay Capital Gains Tax on these distributions.* Unlike your own portfolio, where you have control over your Capital Gains Tax liabilities, these will come without warning. To rub salt into the wound, they may even come at a time when the actual value of your units has declined.

Is There Any Other Way I Can Diversify?

An alternative to managed funds is to buy shares in one of the listed companies that deals in shares – for example, Argo Investments or Australian Foundation. These companies are highly liquid and pay franked dividends. Of course, like the managed funds, they pay administration and other costs that will cut into your profit. There may also be a greater Capital Gains Tax liability as companies pay full tax on gains. They don't, however, include payments to advisers as part of their cost structure.

Caution: Tax Law Is Always Changing

When any product is recommended to you on the basis of its taxation advantages, always keep in mind that these can change at any time. There is no greater proof of this than the constant changes made to superannuation since 1983. Taxation is designed to raise money while pushing you in the direction that the government wants you to go. Remember, the amount of revenue a government needs to raise and the direction in which they want you to go can change very quickly, particularly after you are already committed.

To Summarise

I'm not advising you against managed funds. I'm merely saying to be careful and to *examine a number of options. Don't be rushed into making any decision. It's your life, your money, and you who have to live with the consequences of the decisions that you make.*

In this chapter I have also felt it important to redress, in some small way, the imbalance that currently exists with respect to the promotion of managed funds. Never forget these are strongly promoted by people who have a vested financial interest in you investing with these funds.

6

WHO'S THE RIGHT BROKER FOR YOU?

Stockbrokers are the only agents who can buy and sell shares on the Stock Exchange, so somewhere along the line you will need a broker to act for you.

Broadly speaking, brokers are divided into two categories: *those who give advice and those who simply carry out instructions.* Brokers who give advice are called *'full-service'* brokers, while those who simply carry out instructions are called *'discount'* or *'transaction'* brokers.

Generally, full-service brokers don't charge for the advice they give, but they charge higher commissions on transactions than those charged by discount brokers. This is because full-service brokers incur costs researching the market, going over your portfolio and examining your individual needs.

It follows that full-service brokers must justify their higher fees by giving advice that makes more money for you than you could achieve without that advice. It's a fruitless exercise paying someone to equal what you could achieve yourself or, worse, paying a premium for advice that loses you money.

Keep in mind that brokers receive commissions regardless of the quality of their advice. In my experience, the greater your knowledge the sounder the advice is. If you use a discount broker you're totally relying on your own research and knowledge.

> ### YOU CAN PAY HEAPS – AND STILL GET THE WRONG ADVICE
>
> A broker rang me and advised me to switch from BHP into Transurban. At that stage BHP was about $14 and Transurban was $2000 per share. At that time I was concentrating on weaning my foals, and I agreed without giving his proposal enough attention. BHP thereafter rose above $20 while Transurban failed to get its transponders and tunnel going, and the share price sank to below $1600. I'd been given very poor advice, which left me substantially out of pocket.

> ### BUT IT SOMETIMES PAYS TO LISTEN…
>
> My current broker advised me to sell some Woolworths instalment warrants and invest the proceeds in an Internet stock that I had never heard of. After some research I made the move, which proved financially rewarding (even after the April 2000 high-tech crash).
>
> Unfortunately, while I was doing the research the stock went up by nearly a dollar – so much for my advice about doing your own research!

Just because some brokers concentrate on transactions doesn't necessarily mean that they do these well. Many discount brokers have inadequate systems that make it difficult to place orders – that is, their telephone lines are inadequate or their computer systems frequently go down.

> ### LEFT ON HOLD – WHILE STOCKS SOARED
>
> I once tried to place a telephone order with a very large discount broker. The line was always engaged. Eventually, I was placed in a queue with canned music and a recorded message. By the time I got through, the stock had risen by far more than the commission I was saving, and the whole exercise turned into a Fawlty Towers farce. They later told me this only happened when they were busy!

It's not always easy to find a broker who caters efficiently to your needs. As you'll probably have concluded by now, I've spent a lot of time looking for the ideal broker myself. I'll tell you more about my trials later in this chapter (see page 79).

Choosing a Broker

There are no hard and fast rules for choosing brokers or, as they are termed, 'client advisers'. They all are salespeople. They will all be pleasant and persuasive. Many years ago I was impressed by a prominent Melbourne stockbroker who spun tales of his astute purchases. Unfortunately, when it came to changes in my portfolio his 'gift' deserted him. It's very easy to be an expert in hindsight.

WHAT DO YOU WANT FROM A BROKER?

Think hard about what you really want from a broker. How much advice do you think you need? Do you want guidance on more than just share investment? How much research are you prepared to do yourself?

Things have changed a lot in the last ten years. My first broker nearly fainted when I asked if he had an annual report for a dodgy company he was trying to push onto me. Now, on the Internet, on TV and in print, you are overwhelmed with information.

Full-service brokers have an obligation to ask you about your personal circumstances and needs. Specifically, they should find out whether you are interested in income or long-term growth, the timeframe of your investment horizons, what your tax position is, and how important franking credits are to you. For example, it's no good advising you to buy News Corporation, which pays an annual dividend of 3 cents a share, if you need income. But as a capital growth stock Newscorp has been noted for stellar performance.

TEN QUESTIONS TO ASK BEFORE CHOOSING A BROKER

1. Is the broker interested in you as a client?
2. Is he/she happy to accept whatever amount you propose investing in the market?
3. If so, what kind of philosophy has the broker in relation to sharemarket diversification and risk?
4. What is his/her experience? How long has he/she been with the firm, and what, if any, qualifications has he or she?
5. What research does the firm provide? (Request examples.) Is this research only available to sponsored clients?
6. How accessible is the broker? Will he/she be contacting you – and if so, how often? Too often can be as bad as too little. My disastrous first broker rang me every day, and a friend of mine had the same experience. His broker rang at least once a day, suggesting he buy or sell various stocks. My friend was flattered and excited until he realised he had lost $20,000 in six months!
7. Does the broker have access to new floats? And if so, will he/she give you access to those floats?
8. What are the brokerage rates, including minimum brokerage (this can range from $15 to $100 per transaction).
9. Does the firm arrange client seminars?
10. What arrangements does the firm require you to make for payment of the account?

Always see more than one broker before deciding, and ask each of them for a model portfolio. The quality, quantity and timing of the research you receive will vary dramatically. Don't be sucked in by glossy reports that arrive long after the stock has taken off. *At a later stage, compare the recommendations with what has actually happened.* Keep in mind that, as a small client, you will inevitably receive advice substantially later than the professional market has received it.

> **OOPS! BANK ADVICE WAS BAD ADVICE**
> Some years ago at an ASX open day I collected sample research reports from a prominent brokerage firm. These reports were six months old and were obviously being given out as a cost-saving measure. Had the broker actually looked at what was being distributed I imagine he would have burned the lot. Among other pieces of disastrous advice was a 'sell' recommendation on Commonwealth Bank, which by the time of reading had risen more than 30%.

The type of broker you choose will also depend on the nature of the transaction. If you know you want to buy 500 Coles Myer shares, then you should do this as cheaply as possible. Coles Myer doesn't usually have a huge trading range and, with such a small number of shares, brokerage costs are very important.

On the other hand, if you need complex advice on unfamiliar stocks you should look for a full-service broker. There is no reason why you shouldn't have both, but I object to the practice of getting advice from a full-service broker, then using it to buy stock through a discount broker. It's unfair to the full-service broker and, in any case, in a rapidly changing market you'll need the broker to monitor the stocks he or she recommends to you.

The Saga of My Search for a Broker

You can take many different approaches to finding the right broker – whether by:
- personal recommendation
- attending a stockmarket open day
- making appointments with a series of brokers
- scouring newspaper advertisements
- following stock exchange recommendations.

I tried them all in my quest for Ms or Mr Right, but as you'll see, it wasn't always plain sailing. Anyway, I hope you'll benefit from the numerous mistakes I made along the way! Here is my own rather dismal story.

THE PERSONAL RECOMMENDATION FROM HELL

For once, my ever-reliable cousin wasn't much help here. 'Brokers are,' he explained to me 'about on the level of used car salesman, and the one I use is only the best of a bad bunch.' Undeterred (surely my cousin was only being cynical), I received a recommendation from a 'captain of industry'. Now the broker he suggested may have been wonderful for a very experienced investor, but for me he was a disaster. This was my first broker and I failed to shop round, feeling that, because the person who recommended him was so highly placed, I had some sort of inside running – for which I was privileged to pay top dollar.

Perhaps I should have been suspicious when this highly recommended broker asked me to bring in proof of the amount of money I had to invest – but I was naive. On viewing my bank statement his eyes lit up like the proverbial Christmas tree. It was only later that I realised his request was very unusual – no other broker has ever asked me for such 'proof'.

Apart from that, we basically started off on the wrong foot. I was thinking number of shares and he was thinking amounts of money. I asked him to buy National Australia Bank shares. He did this, but only in proportion, moneywise, to other stock. In other words, instead of buying me 5000 NAB shares he bought me $5000 *worth* of NAB shares – two very different things. He also bought me $5000 worth of other stocks that I had very little interest in. Indeed, I later took a complete aversion to them.

Since this firm later 'disappeared' I can only assume that he saw me as a great opportunity to '*churn*'. Churning is when you buy and sell stocks for the sake of turning them over. The more you churn a client the more commission you make. As I said in the introduction, he was at the time the only person ringing me daily. I was very vulnerable and his attentions made me feel important. But our relationship was doomed.

Among the portfolio of stars he had purchased for me were 10,000 Pioneer International, which he euphemistically referred to as a 'recovery' stock. In fact they kept 'recovering' for ten years till they became a takeover stock. Later this broker suggested I buy 'some more' Pioneer. I thought he meant another few thousand, and agreed. I nearly fainted when I received the contract note and found he had bought me another 10,000, taking my total holdings to 20,000 shares.

I rang around a number of other brokers to find out what they thought of the stock. Without exception they were all negative on it (and as it turned out they were right). Here I was sitting on a great pile of speculation, when what I'd wanted was to be sitting on a great pile of NAB shares (then priced at $7.50).

Sometimes if a broking firm has a large sell order they will push clients into buying that stock so they get commission both ways. I have no idea if this is what occurred, but by any yardstick it was a totally inappropriate purchase for me. At this point I figured that enough was enough. I found a discount broker advertised in the *Financial Review* and unloaded the Pioneer and Pacific Dunlops from my portfolio. *Looking at my portfolio, even the discount broker (who didn't give advice) was horrified and suggested I had been both churned and burned.* Later another adviser in the same firm that had pushed the stocks on me was found guilty of criminal charges relating to churning a client, so I suspect this may have been company policy.

A Costly Visit to the Stockmarket Open Day

Deciding I still wanted a full-service broker, I trotted around the various brokers represented at the ASX open day. I fixed on a female adviser who worked for one of the large broking firms. For a while, things went reasonably well. She gave me additional stock in the Woolworths float and her advice seemed sound, despite some wrong tax advice. However, she left the large firm and went to a smaller one. I followed her there and things started to go wrong.

I had been in and out of a miner called Clutha, and the stock was selling at a low price. I rang the broker who said their analysts had just been briefed on that firm, and that I should buy. Later that week I received a panic-stricken call saying to sell because the shares were 'falling out of bed'. I sold, and within two weeks the stock went into receivership! Well, anyone can make a mistake – and at least she called me to sell.

After that there were a number of less spectacular, but still poor, pieces of advice. There was a mediocre float she tried to push me into with an absurd story about how they were reserving stock for their clients – despite overwhelming demand from outside (so overwhelming that the stock listed under the float price!). We reached the end of the road when I remarked on how well a share had done just after we had sold it. 'Oh,' she said, 'I never look at prices after I sell.'

I rather tersely asked her how, if this was the case, she knew what sort of job she was doing. Then started looking for another broker.

In this case my broker's initial 'expertise' had been reliant on the input received from the research facilities of her original firm. *Moral: always be careful when an adviser changes firms.*

Doing The Rounds

A 42-year-old female friend of mine is the financial director of a multinational firm. She and her husband had many property investments and wanted to expand into the sharemarket. Did I know a good stockbroker? Well, no, I had to admit – actually I didn't. I suggested we make appointments to see up to half a dozen brokers, and decide who she felt comfortable with. This was an interesting exercise.

The first young man we saw was clearly the broker's social security person. He spent an hour counselling Ruth on her likely pension entitlements (something she had never thought of before). We crawled out of there laughing but feeling about 110 years old!

The next broker paced round the room shouting and waving a newspaper (which he carefully explained to us was the *Australian Financial Review*). Thereafter he banged the paper on the table whenever he wished to emphasise a point (usually about himself). Definitely not the sort of personality to inspire confidence in my bean-counting friend!

Finally Ruth found a female broker with a well respected and established firm, who gave her profiles to fill out — and generally behaved within Ruth's comfort zone. As I understand it, while brokerage is high, Ruth and her husband are generally satisfied with the service they receive which includes receiving access to popular floats.

Turning to the Newspaper Ads

Most people find a discount broker by combing through newspaper or magazine advertisements. If you follow this path you should send for the literature and examine all the terms and conditions before making a decision. As I mentioned earlier, you can sometimes lose a lot more while waiting on the phone than you save on commission.

You can get the lowest rates of all by using the Internet. The downside is that the broker will often insist you open a cash management account connected with the firm, and agree to be sponsored. This is designed to lock you in. Despite the 48-hour rule, it's hard changing sponsors – and even worse changing bank accounts – so check the fine print. At the time of writing, I have sent three faxes to a well-known discount broker asking to have a holding changed to issuer-sponsorship and it still has not eventuated!

If you are using the Internet be sure you key in the right stock code. It's your responsibility – and your problem – if you get it wrong. Any carelessness could result in you owning stock you have never heard of.

Seeking Guidance From the Stock Exchange

If you telephone the ASX and tell them the amount of money you have to invest they will, on a rotational basis, direct you to three firms. I was recommended to three specific people. The first one was very nice but didn't seem to know the answers to my most basic questions. The second (as I have already mentioned) told me what a killing he had made on various stocks, including Tabcorp, and the third was really sensible. Like a dope, I chose the second one, who immediately advised me to get rid of two of my stocks. Neither of these were super stars, but both went up in value after I sold. I did get modest access to a couple of floats, but overall it wasn't much good.

Among the poor pieces of advice this broker gave me was that BRLHardy was overpriced at $2.17 (it is now over $7.00).

Instead of listening to my grape-growing, wine expert nephew I'd listened to the broker. So much for having confidence in my own research! From all this you'll gather that there is no infallible way to select a broker. Like most things it involves a lot of work and – in my case – a lot of trial and error.

At Last – I Find a Good Broker!

Happily, I finally discovered a broker who has passed some stringent tests. These are:

- *He actively discourages me from selling stock – and doesn't push me to buy.* ('You've got a great portfolio, Robyn.')
- If I'm selling he puts some thought into it, and usually recommends that I sit in the SEATS system rather than selling immediately at best or market (see Chapter 2).
- I have his direct line and he answers his own calls.
- His advice has been sound, including advice on stock I would never have found on my own.
- His firm sends me a computer report every morning, setting out overnight movements, what has happened the day before and what is expected today.
- If I ask for further information it is faxed through immediately.
- There have been no administrative stuff-ups. Contract notes are faxed through as soon as they are executed, followed by a mailed hard copy.
- He has never tried to lock me into the firm, and at times has encouraged me to seek other advice where he feels he can't appropriately advise me (some brokers specialise in specific areas).
- His charges are very competitive, even judged against those of a discount broker.
- He's always able to sensibly answer my questions on what's happening in the market generally, or why a specific stock is behaving in a particular way. If he's not sure he consults the person in his firm who's an expert in the area, and calls me back.

I'm only a small client of this firm (although I might be bigger if he advised me to sell/buy more) and my broker has no idea I am writing a book. But he has my gratitude. Without him not only would this chapter have had a very bleak ending, but my portfolio would also be the poorer.

To Sum Up

My best advice is: decide what's important to you and keep looking till you find a broker you're happy with, and who comes close to passing my acid tests. If you're using a discount broker — either by telephone or over the Internet — make sure you give the correct instructions.

There is no broker who will be right all the time. The best you can hope for is one who is more often right than wrong — and that when he or she *is* right it is big-time right.

Once again, never forget that a broker's income is derived from the commission obtained through buying and selling your stock.

7

WHAT MAKES THE MARKET RISE OR FALL?

It may puzzle you that one day shares are worth a certain amount and the next their value has either significantly increased or decreased. Why are there such violent and rapid swings? Always remember that when you buy a share you are buying a stake in the *future profits of a company*, and these profits depend on overall economic growth and an individual company's performance. More importantly, the value of shares depends on people's beliefs about future directions of the economy and individual companies.

The Herd Mentality

What basically moves the market are *perceptions about the future*. Present performance and circumstances are taken into account only in so far as they relate to expectations about future performance. No one can be certain what a share in a company will be worth at any given time in the future, so analysts are employed to make predictions.

Forecasting is difficult at the best of times – and almost impossible in uncertain times – and this is why the market loathes uncertainty. When faced with a potential problem the market will factor in a worst- or best-case scenario, depending on the prevailing mood. It's a herd mentality, driven by fear or greed, with no one wanting to be the odd one out. This is especially true of the large institutional investors, whose performances are usually judged against those of its peers.

The underlying philosophy is that it doesn't really matter if you are doing badly, as long as everyone else is doing worse. Sometimes the mood is wildly optimistic, so all news is viewed through rose-coloured glasses. At other times, even positive news is looked on as terribly depressing.

> ### Oil Prices Soared – Fuelled by Fear
> In 1990, when Iraq invaded Kuwait, world stockmarkets plummeted. The price of oil skyrocketed on fears that oil supplies would be decimated, or worse, be controlled by Iraq. After the bombing of Iraq, stock prices rebounded in a frenzy. Initially, investors had factored in a doomsday finale, rather than the most likely outcome.

The emotional responses that often rule the market mean that share prices may reach levels that can't be justified on a rational financial basis. Of course this is never said. Usually 'mum and dad' investors are cautioned not to panic (after the market-makers have precipitated the drop in the first place). The Australian market is divided into two basic categories: the industrial sector and the resources sector. These sectors are influenced by very different considerations. First of all we'll look at what affects the industrial sector.

How Inflation Hurts Your Industrial Shares

The overall worst single nightmare for the industrial sector of the stockmarket (and for you as an investor) is *inflation and its consequences*. Inflation is the rate at which *prices* for goods and services *grow*. Essentially, it means a drop in purchasing power, so there's too much money chasing too few assets. Because we're always looking into the future, it's not a strong current economy which fuels the stockmarket, it's the *potential for growth*. The greater the potential for growth, the greater the scope for corporate earnings to grow. Whether or not economic growth is sustainable depends to a large extent on whether inflation is rising or falling. There is very little potential for growth when the economy is overheated or steaming along at full capacity. The sharemarket anticipates *future* events — which is why the market can surge during a recession and drop during a boom. Remember, *the stockmarket is always moving ahead of the economy*.

CHECK FOR THESE SIGNS OF INFLATIONARY PRESSURE

Generally, rising inflation means *rising employment, rising commodity prices, overheated consumption, and rising asset prices.* Rising wages and commodity prices — and in particular rising oil prices — increase company costs. These increases inevitably lead to lower profits or higher prices. Consumers bid up the price of assets (usually using borrowed money) in the belief that rising inflation will raise the price of these assets even further.

Egged on by over-enthusiastic lending institutions, this leads to financial over-commitment, both by consumers and corporations. As a consequence, if our exports become too expensive to be competitive, or too many imports are sucked in, a balance of payments problem occurs — and individuals and the nation spiral into debt. This scenario, or the prospect of it, inevitably means that *the central banks will increase interest rates* to dampen down the economy. Unfortunately, this can then turn into the recessions 'we have to have'.

HOW HIGH INTEREST RATES AFFECT YOU, THE INVESTOR

A rise in interest rates makes investors — and consumers — cautious. When interest rates are high, many investors tend to switch into safe high-yielding fixed interest or cash securities. With fewer people wanting company shares, prices will fall to reflect lack of demand. Frequently, other consumer expenditure is fuelled by high stockmarket prices. This is called the 'feel rich factor'. We look at the total value of our portfolios and feel rich. Conversely, when share prices decline, share owners immediately feel poorer — even though their losses are still on paper. If consumers borrow on the basis of inflated share prices, and then a fall occurs, confidence is severely dinted — as well as the capacity to repay. And, with a lag, other asset classes including real estate and collectables follow the sharemarket down.

How High Interest Rates Affect Companies

All companies borrow money. When interest rates rise the cost of servicing loans also rises. The more a company has borrowed, the bigger the impact. And the less consistent the cash flow of the company, the more difficult it will be to repay the loan. This is pretty easy to grasp if you think of your own situation. When interest rates rise you have more to pay off your home loan, and the greater your mortgage the greater the difficulty in finding the extra money. When faced with this situation companies do what we all do – pull our horns in. They cut expenditure and postpone or abandon plans for expansion. At the same time, consumers stop buying, so there is less demand for goods – and inevitably bad debts increase.

Low interest rates work in reverse, but always keep in mind that *it's the expectation of future interest rates that moves the market – not the currently prevailing rate.*

All stocks suffer but some stocks are more affected than others.

At a time when interest rates are on the rise some stocks are more badly impacted than others. As a general class these are called 'interest-rate sensitive' stocks.

For a number of reasons banks, which were the standout stock of the '90s (as interest rates declined) are in this category. Investors often choose bank stocks for their yield, that is, for the dividends they pay. (They buy the bank rather than putting their money in the bank.) When outside interest rates rise, yield stocks become less attractive compared to fixed interest securities. In an inflationary environment, assets rise more quickly than inflation. The banks, of course, don't have much in the way of assets. They deal in money, which in an inflationary environment is a depreciating commodity.

Bank profits are produced largely on profit margins derived from borrowing money from one person and lending it to someone else. When interest rates are rising banks have to pay you more to deposit your money, but it is not transparent how they have constructed their loan books. Their profitability will depend on how well they have spread the risk of borrowing and lending, and this will not be known until their actual profit results are released. Competition between banks and other lenders may mean that these margins are very depressed. This of course is the reason the banks are moving to increase their fee income.

The quality of the loan book is another consideration. Will customers be able to repay the loans if interest rates rise? Again, I hope that, in the banks' desire to compete for business, the quality of the loan book won't be compromised. It was in the '80s, which makes it much less likely to occur again. In these times the more responsible the borrower, the less likely they are to borrow – compounding the bank's problems. Institutions don't like these risks, and tend to dump bank stocks as a matter of principle when interest rates are expected to rise. *From a small investor's point of view, this may be a time to buy the banks.*

Other interest rate-sensitive stock are property trusts and insurance stocks – the latter also tending to have large equity portfolios of their own.

A Special Category: Dot Coms

Having soared on a wave of greed and blind optimism, the high-tech stocks were dumped by a wave of fear. Because the companies are highly speculative, they were always vulnerable to a change in market sentiments. Most of the high-tech companies are generating little or no income, have debts and are chewing through their cash at a fast rate ('burn rate'). Neither their shareholders nor the bankers are keen to supply them with more cash – so inevitably many of them will run out of money. This means they'll have to merge with other stronger companies, or submerge altogether.

How Can I Judge Whether Inflation Is Looming?

Even economists disagree on this, and I am not an economist – which some would say makes me eminently qualified to comment! The way I see it, if commodity prices (particularly oil), wages, consumer spending, employment and our balance of payments debt are all on the up it seems pretty likely that this will soon be reflected in the Consumer Price Index, our official monitoring index. If the CPI rises, or looks likely to rise above certain limits, our Reserve Bank will slow the economy down by increasing official interest rates.

What Affects Resource Shares?

The resource sector is export-oriented and prices are largely determined by overseas conditions. When overseas economies are booming the demand for our raw materials is pushed up and share prices rise. When overseas markets contract our shares suffer accordingly. A low-value Australian currency will make our exports cheaper and more competitive.

Australia is a very large gold exporter, and recently gold prices have sunk to all-time lows. This has largely been caused by the gold-selling activities of the world's central banks (including the Reserve Bank). Every time the gold price rises more gold is sold into the market by the banks. This has not helped either our balance of payments or our resources sector. Interestingly, the gold price will often go up in inflationary times as, particularly in the past, this metal has been used as a 'hedge' against inflation. Now the United States dollar ('the greenback') tends to have replaced gold as a hedge.

REMEMBER: WE'RE PART OF A GLOBAL VILLAGE

Australia can't be looked at in a vacuum. The American market accounts for 52%, so it is no wonder that when America sneezes we – and the rest of the world – catch cold. A large drop in the Dow Jones Index or on the Nasdaq Exchange will see a chain reaction round the world, as each stockmarket opens. What causes these large falls usually revolves around inflation and its consequences. Of course other factors, such as a war, an oil crisis, the American president's sexual activities, or the potential break-up of Microsoft, also impact on the market.

Any form of political instability in a key market will have a major impact on its economy and on the companies that operate there. The problems experienced in 1998 in most Asian countries are a good example of this. Other countries' political problems can have a devastating effect. For example, New Guinea's Bouganville was the world's largest copper mine until political insurrection closed it. Years on, the mine is still closed and the shares in it are virtually worthless.

Even in a Slump, 'Super' Steams On

Worldwide, countries are encouraging citizens to save for their retirement.

In Australia we have a system of compulsory employer superannuation contributions, combined with taxation incentives for individual superannuation contributions. This means a lot of new money is coming onto the market looking for a home. Superannuation funds need franking credits to increase their after-tax returns, which suggests that even in a severe downturn they will still hold and buy those companies that are growing and, most importantly, producing franked dividends. A company's ability to pay franked dividends will therefore continue to have a major impact on its share price. Since the banks pay higher franked dividends than most other companies – provided these are maintained – their shares will continue to be the foundation of most superannuation funds.

Despite the availability of franking credits, the raising or lowering of company tax rates will still affect companies' share prices and the amount of profit they can distribute.

Other Factors that May Slow the Market

- Election speculation (a less business-friendly government)
- Budget speculation (unfriendly tax changes)
- Natural disasters (droughts, floods, cyclones, etc.)
- Current account problems

Specific Factors that Can Influence Individual Stocks

Apart from the risks that impact on all stocks there are many events that can affect the value of individual stocks. These include:

- Legal action taken against a company – for example, allegedly faulty pacemaker leads sold by Pacific Dunlop in the USA, or Burns Philp being sued over its role in Estate Mortgage.
- Perceived quality of management. This was a big problem for the Big Australian (BHP) before it replaced most of its board and senior executives. It was also a headache for Coles Myer prior to staff and board changes – not to mention the recent problems at AMP.
- Dilution factors that decrease earnings per share (rights issues, placements, bonus shares options).
- Product quality: Garibaldi was not a public company but its contaminated meat sent it into liquidation.
- Company debts compared to assets – particularly unexpected debts like those faced by the reinsurance arm of GIO.
- Forced selling by shareholders, who have over-borrowed to buy shares.
- End-of-financial-year tax-loss selling.
- Exclusion from one of the major stock indices.
- An increased supply of shares coming onto the market, e.g. vendor shares being released after the escrow period.
- Market momentum. If one institution starts buying or selling the others will jump on and move the stock, followed by private investors not wanting to either be caught or miss out.
- A well-known analyst publishing a strong up- or down-grading of a company can trigger momentum.
- New competitive pressures on a company.
- When a share is considered under- or over-valued.

- Share buy-backs. These can positively affect your portfolio by decreasing the number of shares on issue.
- The perception that a stock has become a takeover target. When another company wants to buy an existing business they have to pay a premium over the current share price (but they will often launch these bids when the share price of the target company is at a low point).
- Pure fashion: certain stocks become 'market darlings' – and investors are very optimistic.
- Some good company news, unexpected by the market.

When Is a Share Too Expensive?

I often hear my students say that a share costs too much because its price is more than $20. But this is like saying a house is too expensive without looking at what you are actually buying for the money. Whether a company is expensive or not depends not on its actual price but on what its earnings and prospects are. One of the measures that analysts use to value companies is the price earnings ratio.

Get to Know the Price Earnings Ratio (PER)

As I've explained, a company's share price rises or falls depending on how fast its earnings are expected to increase. Comparing a share's price with its earnings shows how quickly investors expect these profits to increase. *This ratio indicates the number of times the market value of the shares exceeds its earnings per share.* A price-to-earnings ratio is calculated by dividing a company's share price by its annual earnings per share.

Formula:

$$\text{PER} = \frac{\text{current share value}}{\text{earnings per share}} \quad \text{e.g.} \quad \frac{\$20}{\$1} = \$20$$

This means that *if earnings remain static it will take 20 years for your annual earnings to pay for the cost of the share*. It follows that it is not expected that earnings will remain static but are expected to increase. Unfortunately, this calculation is not entirely accurate. While the share price will always be up to date, the earnings will either be historical (as published in the newspapers) or the result of a forecast, which is constantly subject to revision and may be right or wrong. The best way to use this ratio is by comparing the PERs of companies in similar sectors. If a company has a very high or very low PER compared to other similar companies, you need to know why. The higher the PER the higher the optimism about the stock.

If analysts are factoring in very high growth rates, and these are not achieved, the stock price will plummet. Stocks can be dramatically overpriced so that no matter how good they are, like any other asset, they won't represent investment value. The higher the PER the more vulnerable a stock will be to bad news, as clearly all the potential good news has been well and truly factored in.

Before the April 2000 crash, a number of Internet stocks were selling at PERs of over 300. Needless to say, these thumped back to earth with a resounding bang.

The Internet and high-tech stock are growth areas, but picking the winners from the losers is both daunting and high risk. Remember, it's not just deciding which good idea will actually make it, it's also working out whether the company will have the funds to stay in business – and whether another company will have an even better idea.

Go with the Cash Flow

Look for companies that not only have earnings but also have 'free' cash flow. By this I mean the cash that a company has after it has met its basics commitments – a bit like you looking at what discretionary income you have *after* you have paid the mortgage, etc. The greater the free cash flow (compared to earnings) the greater the capacity for the company to pursue its growth strategy.

The Sylvester Stallones of the Stockmarket

I have a personal theory that is not only sexist but has no statistical backing of any kind. I think of it as the 'testosterone factor'. Put at its simplest, men get bored in an uneventful market. They like to be doing something – and market action gets the adrenalin flowing. Rapid response turns them into 'action men'. Add in the competitive element of beating your rivals and the fear of being left behind – and I think you'll all catch my drift. If my theory has any validity it's really surprising the market is as stable as it is.

8

GETTING STARTED ON YOUR PORTFOLIO

Where do you begin, once you've decided to invest in the sharemarket? Well, you can rush off to a highly recommended stockbroker brandishing your bank statements and tell him to use his best judgement – as I did – or you can sit down and think about what you're really trying to achieve *before* you seek further advice.

Overall, as with any investment, you must look at the cash flow the investment will generate (income) and its likely value at the end of the investment period (capital return). But there are other factors you should think about that are specific to your needs.

First, what is your objective in investing in the sharemarket? The answer, of course, is to make money. But you need to be a bit more specific. *Do you need income and, if so, do you need franking credits? (See page 53.) Or are you looking for long-term growth? Or perhaps you want to balance the two.*

But, I can hear you saying, if shares are classified as growth investments, why do I have to choose between income and growth? In fact, returns on shares come through both *share price appreciation* and through *dividend income*. However, some companies are oriented to capital growth and others to yield income.

The second factor you have to consider is *your timeframe* in investing. Unless you're prepared to commit the money for a significant period of time the sharemarket is not for you.

This doesn't mean that all investments will take time to be profitable — had you bought into Telstra 1 you would have been in profit from day one. Rather, it means that because you're buying the company's future profits, it will need time to generate those profits.

The stockmarket goes up and down. Even though the company you've invested in is performing well, a general market decline may still drag its share price down. When, for example, the gold price sank *all* gold companies fell — including the good, the bad and the ugly. However, a good company will fall less and recover more quickly than an also-ran. *So when a general sector fall occurs, it's usually a good time to buy the best companies in that sector* (provided you can identify them!).

Because share prices fluctuate daily, you never want to be in the position of having to sell by a specific date. *And remember, if you trade shares in the short term you will pay full Capital Gains Tax on assets disposed of within twelve months of acquisition.*

The third factor you need to consider is your attitude to *risk*. We all like to sleep at night so, if risk really worries you, you may be better off putting your money into a cash investment. (Then you'll only have to worry about inflation eroding your capital — or the institution in which you have invested going bankrupt.)

Finally, you need to consider your responsibilities and the financial resources available to you. After all, we're not talking about monopoly money.

Regardless of whether you are looking for growth or income you should be seeking quality stocks — and this means market *dominance of a growth industry*. (It would have been pointless to have been the best buggy whip manufacturer in the early 1900s, because demand for your product was shrinking at a cracking pace.) Conversely, many motor car firms started up in that era, but not many prospered.

Currently this can be compared to the Internet stocks – many are trying but very few will succeed. As with the purchase of any business, you must be prepared to research the activities of the company you are intending to buy. Find out what the positives are for buying into this particular company – excluding hot tips and rumours.

> *I told Grandpa to sell his steamship shares, but he wouldn't listen!*

STEADY AND SLOW: THE 'SAFE' WAY TO GROW

My friend Melly is 51. Her home is paid off and she has a well-paid job. Currently, she doesn't need additional income. She is looking to the future, but is not a risk-taker. Her priority, when she first began investing, was to find a relatively safe growth stock. She was patient, and her first share investment was in the initial Telstra float – an ideal investment for someone wanting a blue-chip growth stock. Telstra is a dominant player in a growth industry generating very healthy profits, but not much in the way of franked dividends. While its share price may fluctuate in the short term, in the long term its earnings and infrastructure should see it grow.

> **HIGH RISK, HIGH GAIN – BUT POSSIBLE PAIN**
> Another friend who has a high tolerance – in fact a positive enjoyment – of risk has a personal portfolio comprised solely of high-technology stocks. For a period of time, they all rose – and her hope was that a least one would succeed. Fortunately, she could afford to lose the money she had invested. But it was still painful and not very exciting when the high-tech stocks collapsed. Hopefully, those in her portfolio will survive and ultimately prosper. Ironically, one of the reasons she failed to lock in her gain was the prospect of paying CGT – not a problem now! In fairness, I should say that her superannuation fund comprises solid blue-chip stocks.

Income Stocks – How Much Do They Pay?

If you want to buy stocks for the income they provide you'll constantly hear the word 'yield' used. Dividend yield is simply the return to an investor expressed as a percentage of the current market price of the share.

Formula:

$$\text{Dividend yield} = \frac{\text{dividend per share}}{\text{share price}} \times 100 = \%$$

e.g.

$$\frac{\text{dividend 50 cents}}{\text{share price \$5}} \times 100 = 10\%$$

You'll note that this equation has the same deficiency as that of the price/earnings ratio: the dividend is either historic or a forecast, while the share price is actual. As the price of the stock rises the yield will fall unless the dividend is also constantly rising. Conversely, as the price of a share drops, provided the dividend remains constant, the yield will increase.

Care must be taken when using this ratio to compare share yields with other forms of investment, as this simple equation fails to take the effects of *dividend imputation* into account. If a dividend is fully franked the yield, when grossed up to take account of the franking credit, will be much higher. You can see from this that a high-yielding stock may be so simply because of a poor share price. If this is the case, it doesn't bode well for the future profitability of the company.

> ### Help! Our Share Prices Are Shrinking!
> I have friends who, as self-funded retirees, are totally dependent on income-earning assets and, in particular, on franked income from shares. Because some companies maintain dividends – even in the face of decreased earnings – the share price of some of their stocks have sunk while the dividend has remained constant. This has made the yield look very good.

My friends are reluctant to quit these stocks, even though they know they're losing capital. They get around this by looking on the shrinking of their stocks as an unrealised rather than a real loss. Like Mr Micawber, they hope something will 'turn up' to boost the stock prices again. But unless earnings per share increase there will come a time when the companies won't be able to pay such high dividends – and my friends will then suffer further capital losses. I'm still trying to persuade them to take the capital situation into consideration and not be blinded by what may well be a temporarily high yield.

> ### My Friend Hit the Jackpot
> Another retired friend needed income to supplement a small pension. She wanted capital growth as well, but it was not her first priority. As it happened, she hit the jackpot by investing in the initial float of the Commonwealth Bank. At the time the share price was $5.40. The bank now sells for more than $27 and pays very high fully franked dividends.

Growth and Income

Both Telstra and the Commonwealth Bank enjoy large profits. But while Telstra reinvests most of its profits in the future growth of the company, the Commonwealth Bank pays out 70% of its earnings as dividends to its shareholders.

The Difference between Earnings and Dividends

Many women in my classes confuse dividends with earnings. The *earnings of a company is the net profit*. To work out earnings per share (EPS) you divide the net company profit by the number of shares on issue.

Formula:

$$\text{EPS} = \frac{\text{net profit}}{\text{number of shares}} \quad \text{e.g.} \quad \frac{\$2000}{2000} = \$1.00$$

Dividends are paid out of earnings, but it depends on company policy how much of a company's earnings is distributed to shareholders and how much is retained by the company to invest in future growth. This is called the *payout ratio*, which is the percentage of earnings that are paid out as dividends.

How to Calculate the Payout Ratio

The CBA pays out approximately 75% of its net earnings to its shareholders as dividends.

Formula:

$$\frac{\text{dividend}}{\text{earnings}} \times 100 = \text{payout ratio} \quad \text{e.g.} \quad \frac{0.75}{\$1.00} \times 100 = 75\%$$

It's a bad sign when a company actually cuts its dividend to shareholders. That's why you should look for a steady or rising dividend sustained over a long period of time. Whether or not you're interested in dividends, they can only be paid out of earnings so it's important that you *look for companies that have a history of steadily rising earnings*.

Companies will usually seek to avoid cutting dividends, and may do this by raising the payout ratio, so you must look at what is happening to the earnings from which the dividend is paid. Earnings can be increased by a company growing its profits, or by a share buy-back, (the fewer the number of shares on issue the higher the earnings per share). Conversely, earnings can be decreased by company growth slowing down or by an increase in the number of shares on issue (dilution) via placements, rights issues, bonus shares, options, etc.

How to Identify Income Stocks – and Growth Stocks

Banking stocks, listed property trusts and utilities are classic income (yield) stocks, while resource stocks, media technology and pharmaceuticals are examples of growth stocks. The Internet, telecommunications, bio-medical and related stocks are 'hot' growth stocks. (They're a long way from being income stocks as they are usually operating at a loss.)

There's no doubt that this technology will change our lives forever, as did the motor car and the aeroplane. But, as with those industries, only a few are going to make it. Remember *the risk and reward equation* when venturing into this area. PERs over 20 are getting to be fully valued and those over 200 show boundless optimism. *Eventually these companies must produce quality earnings or disappear.*

Some Shares Come with 'Goodies' Attached

Of course, one doesn't always buy stock in the hope of making money – there can be quite different objectives. The obvious example is to buy 500 shares in Coles Myer to obtain the discount card. (As I write, this entitles you to a discount at several stores, including 10% at Myer/Gracebrothers, $7\frac{1}{2}$% at Target and K-Mart and 5% at Coles Supermarket and

Liquorland.) I did this several years ago, thinking that $4.30 was a lot to pay for a Coles Myer share. However, they have increased substantially since then. My holding was tiny so I signed up for the dividend reinvestment plan and am now the owner of about 630 Coles Myer shares. By simply reinvesting my dividends I have increased the number of shares I hold by 26%.

Taking the Timeframe into Account

Short-term trading works when the market is rising. Indeed when speculative shares are running, players simply buy on the momentum of a stock, not really caring what that stock is as long as it's 'hot'. However, in a falling or stagnant market, things are very different.

The longer the period of your investment, and the longer the time you need to live off the money, the more certain you need to be about a company's fundamental value — and the more necessary it is that you should invest in growth assets.

I don't agree with advisers who recommend capital-protected investments for those approaching or in their twilight years. If you know you have to retire and move funds on a certain date, of course you should protect your capital, as your timeframe is defined and limited. On the other hand, if — like me — you are over fifty and expect to live another thirty years you have a very long time horizon.

If your investments are in solid companies paying good dividends there's no reason why you shouldn't simply wait out any general market downturn. In this case, choosing the right stocks is very important. If you want to live well then you must have increasing capital assets, and you must monitor those assets. If you have a capital gain that you wish to realise, you may consider offsetting the gain by selling a stock that's currently in a loss situation. If you feel the stock still has growth prospects, you can then repurchase it. This will establish a new and lower cost base for a future disposal.

> ### UNFLAPPABLE AUNT'S WINNING FORMULA
> My aunt has for many years held a portfolio comprised largely of bank stocks. These have enjoyed both capital growth and income. When she has needed additional funds she has sold stock, but because of the rapid rise in price of her stock, she seems to be no worse off capital-wise than she was ten years ago. From time to time she also buys some rather more speculative stocks, but these also have performed very well. She really enjoys following the market and is quite unflappable, even when stocks are heading down.

How Much Risk Are You Comfortable With?

To determine the risk versus the reward, the return from an investment in a growth area should be compared with the return from the no-risk government bond. After doing the sums you decide on the level of risk you feel comfortable with.

Here we are all different. However the spectrum of people I know who invest in shares covers the widest possible range. Perhaps the most conservative is a museum curator – who never gets rid of anything – so Telstra can rest easy about her shares ever being sold.

The person I breed and race horses with has a very high tolerance of risk – and the only thing that saves her from herself is her need for fully franked dividends. This minimises her investments in the speculative shares she would love to have. Ironically, given that racehorses are the most unreliable and high-risk 'investments' in the world, my racehorse trainer was so concerned about the risks of the sharemarket that he refused to buy into Telstra 1! (Or perhaps the horses were going too slowly to fund the investment.)

> ### HOW NOT TO BUY SHARES!
> There's a big difference between taking a calculated risk and being just plain foolish. My friend Jenny falls into the second category. She is geared to the absolute hilt on a penthouse apartment she can't afford. On the casual advice of a neighbour (who had no idea of her circumstances), she took out a bankcard loan to buy some highly speculative Internet shares.

Initially the shares went up but she refused to sell, saying she would wait till they doubled, then sell half. Well, they never did double. Fortunately, she ended up getting her money back, and making a very small profit. On the other hand, this was eroded by brokerage fees. And, because she didn't hold the shares for twelve months, she'll pay full Capital Gains Tax on what little remains, at her full marginal rate. At the time of writing these shares are well below her initial purchase price. *This is gambling, not investing – with a risk totally out of proportion to the return.*

If you have *a high tolerance of risk and can afford to take losses,* by all means have some speculative stock. But before you do, make sure you know what the company does and what its history is. In cases like this I would recommend consulting a stockbroker. Jenny had no idea what the company did – she just wanted to make money. Unfortunately, it's rarely that easy. And never borrow on your credit card to buy shares – the interest rate is simply too great. In Jenny's case, of course, it was the only way she could borrow. It makes the blood run cold!

A Painless Way to Invest

Ideally, as a novice investor, you should actually have the money to pay for your shares, and *be using share purchases as a way of saving for the future. You don't need large sums of money to start investing in the sharemarket.* If you choose companies that have dividend reinvestment and/or share purchase plans you can dribble money in quite painlessly. Alternatively, you can pay an agreed amount monthly into a managed fund.

Borrowing Money to Buy Shares

Borrowing money to buy shares can be workable, provided *you can service the loan, have ample security, it fits with your taxation strategy, and the shares increase in value.* You can borrow against your home, provided it is paid off – if it isn't, this should be your first priority – but this makes me uneasy. We all need a place to live.

The common form of loan used to buy shares is called *a margin lending account*. When you borrow for real estate a value is fixed for the property which is then generally not revalued during the term of the loan, regardless of whether values go up or down (value being subjective until you actually sell). Shares are different – they're constantly being valued. If you borrow, say, 70% of the value of a portfolio and use 30% of your own money you will be expected to maintain that ratio. The shares you can buy will be from a list provided by the lender, which will not include speculative equities.

Suppose you want to buy a portfolio of shares worth $30,000 and borrow 70% of its value ($21,000). Provided the total value of your portfolio remains at $30,000 or above, you will simply be paying interest, and other fees, as with a normal loan. However if your portfolio should drop in value to, say, $27,000 you'll need to top up your loan to retain the 70% ratio. In this case you would have a *margin call* of 10% or $3000. You will then need to put up further securities, pay the amount in cash, or sell some of your shares. None of these alternatives is palatable unless you have sufficient resources to meet the call.

Interest is tax deductible, provided you buy an income-earning asset (that is, a share that pays dividends). *This form of borrowing (called gearing) magnifies the potential for both gains and losses, so be very careful.* Even with a significant 'safety margin', shares can still exceed the margin. In a relatively short period of time NAB shares lost just under 30% of their value, and Telstra 2 has also fluctuated by that amount. When the market drops and a number of margin calls are made, shares will be sold to meet the call, and share prices will be driven even lower. The fall in the share price of Telstra 2 has been exacerbated because not only have people borrowed to buy Telstra itself, they have also borrowed against Telstra shares as collateral to finance more speculative purchases (high-tech stock). These speculative purchases have fallen by up to 80% – so guess what has to be sold! Borrowing to buy shares can work, provided the circumstances are right. *But be cautious!*

> **A Smart Borrower Stays Ahead**
> Ryan has been investing in the sharemarket for many years and has a substantial portfolio of blue-chip shares that have gained significantly in value. He is also paying tax in the top bracket. Ryan uses his portfolio as security to borrow money to buy further shares. The size of his collateral means he will never face a margin call, and the interest he pays reduces his tax bill considerably. Of course, he will need to pay back the loans eventually. (I gather he is working on that.)

Instalment Warrants: the Inside Story

If you have a self-managed superannuation fund you won't be able to borrow to buy investments. In this case – provided it's allowed by the trust deed, and subject to the approval of an adviser – you may consider the use of an instalment warrant. An instalment warrant gives you the right to buy the underlying share by paying an issuer an initial payment of about 60% of the price of the share, and a set balance at a later date. These are called *derivative instruments*, which means they are derived from the price of the underlying share.

Essentially, an institution is lending you the money for the second payment. Depending on whether you buy the warrants on the primary or secondary market the interest component may be tax deductible. (As I write, this is the subject of some debate.)

After being issued by way of an 'Offering Circular' (primary market) these warrants are traded on the ASX (secondary market). The attraction is that all dividends and franking credits are passed on to the investor. On the downside, there is a very illiquid market for these warrants (which means they can't readily be sold), and the issuers themselves largely comprise that market.

So my advice is that you only consider buying warrants if you really want the stock, but haven't got the necessary finance to make an outright purchase. When the balance becomes due you'll usually have the option of either paying or rolling over the warrants into a new issue. Look carefully at the terms of the issue – buying warrants with a small first payment and a large second payment (high-octane warrants) may mean you can buy more, but it will really magnify your losses if the market falls.

'My Portfolio: What Sort of Shares Should I Start With?'

This depends on you. However most advisers would recommend that regardless of whether you want income or growth you start building your portfolio with a carefully chosen range of conservative blue-chip companies. These are likely to include a number of different sectors covering banking, retail, media, resources and telecommunications. Diversification of shares won't protect you from a general market downturn, but it will lessen the risks of having all your eggs in one basket.

In a downturn a good stock will fall less than a speculative one, and generally will recover more quickly. Most importantly, you should really try to understand the business you are buying and consider the reasons you are buying it – a point of view that was foreign to most investors in the dot com market.

Always look at what competitive advantage a company may have – for instance, it would be very difficult for a competitor of Transurban to build a toll tunnel. Ask yourself whether the company has a really strong brand name (for example, Coca-Cola) that makes competition difficult. Whether you want growth or income you want a profitable company.

Here we should look at another ratio called '*return on equity*'. What this identifies is how much profit the company is returning on the funds it has to work with – *in short, what they're doing with your money!* If the company is generating returns below what they (or you) could achieve by sticking the money in the bank, then the company is clearly not using its resources (your money) well. If, on the other hand, its growth is double digit then it would seem to be achieving greater returns on the funds than you'd be able to do.

'How Can I Work Out My Return on Equity?'

Of course, start-up companies don't generate profits, so they can't be judged using this ratio, so it must be applied with discretion.

Formula:

$$\frac{\text{after tax profits}}{\text{shareholders' equity}} \times 100 = \text{return on equity} \quad \text{e.g.} \quad \frac{\$10}{\$100} \times 100 = 10\%$$

Shareholders' equity is the amount that would be returned to shareholders if the company was wound up, and all its debts paid. Whatever you do, try not to achieve too much at once, and resist getting hooked on the 'hype' or the 'despair'. Racecourse experience has taught me that gamblers don't boast about their losses.

Buy into Companies You Know About – and Understand

Scattered around the chapters of this book, I have mentioned some ratios analysts use to examine and predict a company's performance. *But I believe that simple common sense and personal experience are just as important.* As I mentioned earlier, my nephew is a wine expert, but I ignored this fact and took the advice of a stockbroker over his. Since wine is my nephew's livelihood, this was really dumb – he knows a lot more about the industry than any financial analyst.

On a personal level, I believed that the Commonwealth Bank had a lot of room for cost-cutting as long as two branches of this bank faced each other in Watton Street, Werribee. At that stage the share price was under $8 and not being recommended by brokers. This has turned into one of my most profitable investments.

> **I Ignored Harvey Norman – and Kicked Myself Later**
>
> Having finally decided to totally renovate my bathroom, I trudged from shop to shop before buying virtually everything from Harvey Norman. At the same time a friend was looking for a new television set and video and, having gone through a similar exercise, also bought from Harvey Norman. Lamentably, neither of us thought to buy shares in this company. They have since tripled in price.

I recently read an article which mentioned that the writer's mother (who lived in the USA) had invested in Johnson & Johnson thirty years ago, because she thought their Band-Aids were so good. She has done very well out of Band-Aids!

It seems to me that nearly everything you do in life can be used as a marketing research exercise. If you're looking at a stock, think about current and future competition. A good example of this is the competition facing Telstra in all its traditional markets. Here the weight of money is with Telstra, but competition can happen in any industry. For example, Biota spent years developing a flu drug called Relenza. It did all the right things and had a strong American partner (Glaxo). The share price climbed above $9 when the drug was released for the northern hemisphere winter. Unfortunately, Relenza was delivered via an inhaler, and another drug company (Roche) produced a flu drug in tablet form. Biota and its partner are now trying to persuade the 70% of Americans who chose the tablet that inhalers are preferable. Meanwhile the Biota share price has slid below $3. Which would *you* be most likely to buy – an inhaler or a tablet?

Other research includes reading as much as you can about the economy and particular stock, but we will go into this in detail in Chapter 10. Be very careful buying speculative stock when you don't understand what the company does. It may be a winner or it may be pie in the sky. Only invest money you can afford to lose in these stocks.

The Buck Stops with You

No matter how competent your broker, it's you who must make the final decision, and it's also you who profits or loses from the investment. A core portfolio of shares in large, dominant companies with steady earnings growth that are readily marketable will stand you in good stead despite the ups and downs of the market. Speculative shares can give you a great return but can also cause you great losses. Don't get caught up in market mania. Be aware of your own tolerance of market movements; don't let your own mood be a reflection of that currently prevailing on the stockmarket.

> **GRANDPA WAS A SHARE BAROMETER**
> A friend's grandfather was a keen market investor. Without a word being exchanged my friend could tell how the stockmarket was performing by the look on his grandfather's face each evening.

Don't be intimidated by analyst ratios. Remember, they are for the most part only guides and are based on either forecast or historical data. Try to think of the rationale behind them – *it all comes down to trying to ascertain how well the business is performing and is expected to perform*. On top of that, don't imagine for one moment that the market (despite all the ratios) is rational. The market may be many things but being rational is not usually one of them.

A word of warning: be very careful when applying newspaper articles written about the American stockmarket to Australia. The United States doesn't have our rules relating to franking credits and has a very low Capital Gains Tax. Consequently, American companies are focused on capital growth rather than paying dividends. This is illustrated by Newscorp, which is essentially an American company. At the time of writing, its dividend per annum is about 3 cents, on a share price of about $21.

9

BUILDING YOUR PORTFOLIO

Once you've decided which shares you're interested in buying, and have organised your finances, you must decide when you'll buy and, later on, when you'll sell. One thing that will become clear is that *there is no such thing as the perfect time to buy or sell*. I've had students who faithfully follow share prices but somehow never feel the time is right to invest. What they are looking for is the perfect moment to invest – but this is unrealistic.

While it's depressing to buy a share and immediately see it go down – or conversely, not to buy and see the price rocket – a good share will remain a good share. Provided it doesn't get too expensive, it will ride the ups and downs. As I have emphasised before, one of the most difficult things is to resist the hype and the temptation to rush in to buy as the market is peaking – and conversely not to sell because the bubble has burst and it is all doom and gloom.

They Don't Ring a Bell when it's Time to Sell

It's easy to say 'buy low and sell high'. But, not surprisingly, timing the market is very difficult – despite what the sellers of various computer systems may assert. A well-known saying in the stockmarket is that 'no one rings a bell to tell you when the market has reached its high or low' – which is a way of saying that picking the exact high and low points is virtually impossible. According to another old stockmarket expression, you should 'leave something for the next person'. Taking this admonition to heart, I've often left rather too much for the next person. It can be really confusing. On the one hand, market 'experts' assert that you 'never go broke taking a profit', while others say you should 'let your profits run'. So how do you reconcile this apparently conflicting advice? And what factors should you take into account?

Think Medium to Long-term

It's easy to see when the indices are at high points, and when an individual share price is at or near its high or low. But what you don't know is whether the whole market is going to keep on climbing or retreat, or whether an individual share will keep moving up or is about to sink. You'll go mad if you let yourself become obsessed by this. *Remember that the medium to long-term growth of earnings per share is the key factor.* You're buying the *future profits* of the company, so these should be growing at a sustainable pace into the foreseeable future. I've already discussed earnings per share and the price/earnings ratio (PER). When the PER gets into the mid-twenties shares are looking expensive, and when they reach over 200 they are unsustainably expensive.

'Should I Buy Shares With or Without their Dividend?'

If income isn't a priority you can buy shares more cheaply shortly after they go ex-dividend, and then wait six months for your first dividend. Conversely, by buying a share just before it goes ex-dividend you can get three dividend payments in thirteen months. This is because dividends are paid every six months and, by receiving an immediate dividend, you reduce the waiting period. Which approach you choose to adopt will depend on your circumstances and finances. If you have less money you may buy ex-dividend; if you want franking credits you may buy with the dividend.

In either case, always be aware whether a company has declared a dividend and when it goes ex-dividend. Every Monday the *Australian Financial Review* has details of all dividends that have been declared but not paid. The same goes for any other entitlements a share may be carrying – for example, a rights or bonus share issue.

Consider 'Dripping' when the Market's Dipping

One method of buying is to wait until the market dips, which you can be certain it will, and start dripping money in. You can't ignore brokerage costs – the very minimum is $15 for a transaction over the Internet, ranging up to more than $100 with a full-service broker. So dribbling in too small an amount of money can be very expensive. There are two specific drip methods: averaging up and averaging down.

AVERAGING UP

If you buy a particular stock and the price goes up you continue to feed money in to subsequent purchases. This means that your average price for the stock will increase, but the idea is that the share price will increase even more.

> **AVERAGING UP CAN PAY OFF – DESPITE RISING PRICES**
>
> My cousin and I started chasing a stock in a small illiquid company. My first purchase was 10,000 at 29 cents. After that I bought four more lots of 10,000 at prices of 31 cents, 32 cents, 38 cents and 42 cents – giving me an average price of 34 cents. The last share sale for this stock was 55 cents, so I am reasonably happy. My cousin went on to acquire far more than I did – using this method – and is currently *very* happy. Of course it would have been nice to have acquired all my stock at 29 cents but this was not possible. In this case there were very limited amounts of shares coming onto the market, and the share price was constantly rising. At other times you may want to limit your commitment or you may not have the financial resources for a one-off purchase.

Averaging Down

As the term suggests, this is the reverse of 'averaging up'. Each time the share price slides lower you buy more, decreasing your average cost per share. This is done in the expectation (or hope) that over time the share price will once again rise above your average price. Unfortunately this approach can often misfire — and become a case of throwing good money after bad.

There's a saying in the horse world that horses neither know nor care what price you paid for them — and people rarely hang on to duds in the hope that they'll come good. Of course, unlike a share, it costs money to keep a horse — which makes people far more pragmatic. Nevertheless, a share doesn't know what you paid for it either, and you should have a more compelling reason for hanging on to stock or increasing your holding than a reluctance to admit that you were wrong in your initial purchase. But perhaps I am too quick to cut my losses.

> **Averaging Down Can Be Risky…**
> When Burns Philp was sinking without trace from more than $2 to below 20 cents a well-known radio personality was advising listeners to average down — at least he did until the stock sank below a dollar. Given the company's crippling debt level, this advice was very optimistic. Of course, if you'd waited till the shares bottomed at below 20 cents you would subsequently have made a profit. But that is bottom-trawling rather than averaging down.

Look Out for the Warning Signs

In the above example, before Burns Philp's share price collapsed under a sea of debt, the company had a legal action against it over its trusteeship of Estate Mortgage. I won't go into details here, but on examination it was apparent the company should have settled this action. The fact that they let it roll on indicated either a lack of judgement on the part of management, or a lack of money to settle the case – hardly the hallmarks of a well-run company in either case. This should have sent a red flag to investors. Likewise, the problems Crown Casino was having with its building program should have signalled that all was not well with the company.

If you remember back to the crash of 1987, it was crippling debt that sank the entrepreneurs. Basically, bad business decisions – particularly relating to acquisitions – had been responsible for increasing companies' exposure to debt. And it's this that has caused the grave problems suffered by a number of blue-chip icons.

So before you start averaging down you should look at the company's financial strength and its debt level. While earnings per share occupy centre-stage in valuing companies, their debt levels, compared to their assets and cash flow, are also very important – just as they are in our own personal finances.

Make Sure You Know What Companies Owe

I've already talked about a company's ability to service its debts. A company with a good cash flow can cope with a higher level of debt than a company with an uncertain cash flow. However any company overburdened with debt must be looked at with some trepidation, particularly if interest rates seem set to rise. There are ratios that examine debt levels, though once again they have their limitations.

'How Do I Calculate the Debt-to-Equity Ratio?'

This ratio simply looks, in percentage terms, at the amount of debt a company has – *compared to its total assets or shareholders' equity* (the amount of your money left after all debts have been paid). To be strictly accurate the debts involved should be those on which the company has to pay interest.

Formula:

$$\frac{\text{interest-bearing debt}}{\text{shareholders' equity}} \times 100 = \text{debt-to-equity ratio} \quad \text{e.g.} \quad \frac{\$100}{\$50} \times 100 = 50\%$$

In this example 50% of the company assets are consumed by debt. The higher this figure the more concerned you should be. If it goes over 100% it is seriously worrying. The better the cash flow the more comfortable a high ratio is, so you would expect a company like Woolworths to be able to comfortably carry more debt than, say, a junior mining company. Of course, high debt levels are worse if interest rates are rising, even though interest payments are tax deductible.

'...And How Do I Work Out Net Tangible Assets?'

Another ratio used to determine a company's worth is its *net tangible assets per share (NTA)*. This calculates the value of the tangible assets remaining after all the liabilities have been paid. Because this figure only looks at *tangible* assets there's no point in applying it to those firms whose prospects are based on intangible assets. Intangibles include brainpower (the best assets often walk out the door each night) and goodwill from strong brand names (magazine titles, labels, etc.). It also assumes a price based on book values which may not be accurate and which may change over the six months reporting period.

Formula:

$$\frac{\text{shareholders' equity} - \text{intangible assets}}{\text{number of shares}} = \text{NTA} \quad \text{e.g.} \quad \frac{\$500}{100} = \$5$$

In the above example, each share has a theoretical tangible asset backing of $5. But in a forced disposal, asset values may not be realised, while in other cases assets may be undervalued (for example the value of property held may have risen).

Where a company invests in other listed companies the NTA is a moveable feast. So while this ratio has some interest you should not buy a share based solely on its net tangible assets being below its current share price.

Looking at the economy and at an individual company's assets and performance is called *fundamental analysis*. The major alternative to this is to use *technical analysis* or *charting*.

'How Accurate is Charting or Technical Analysis?'

Chartists believe that all the information about a stock is already built into the stock price and that future prices can be predicted by examining past share prices and buying and selling volumes. Their mantra is 'the trend is your friend' – that is, you follow market momentum to make buying and selling decisions.

There are some complicated formulae associated with this system (which is also known as technical analysis – as opposed to fundamental analysis, which looks at actual company performance). If everyone believed the chartists' basic theory it would become a self-fulfilling prophecy, but not everyone does believe. A company's past share price is interesting – you do need to know where it has been, and what volumes are driving the price – but it's debatable whether all factors are known and built into a perfectly functioning market.

Before the computer age, charting involved copying down and graphing prices of shares. These days, most sites give you share prices, and provide graphs of a share's historic price movements.

Another difficulty I have with charting is that, while it appears scientific, the sharemarket is an inexact science with a lot of movement being psychologically motivated. I'm not convinced that this factor can be built into any model. Unfortunately, a lot of computer systems are currently being sold which make grandiose claims about the ability of that system to predict the market. Like everything else, let the buyer beware. If the systems were as good as they're cracked up to be the promoters would become rich using rather than selling them!

'Should I Buy in Gloom and Sell in Boom?'

Some people believe in investing in out-of-favour stocks when prices are depressed. In other words, they go against the prevailing trend. This 'contrarian' theory is best illustrated by the phrase 'buying straw hats in winter'. However, you shouldn't rush in and buy a share just because it has fallen in price. Always find out *why* it has fallen in price, and then make a considered judgment as to whether or not the price is likely to recover. A popular saying, as I write, is 'Don't try to catch a falling knife'. In other words, it's dangerous to buy stocks when prices are rapidly falling.

'How Big Should My Portfolio Be?'

This is really up to you. Again, there are conflicting maxims. 'Don't not put all your eggs in one basket' versus 'Put most of your eggs in one basket and watch that basket carefully'.

As a matter of personal preference, I have about three core stocks that I have taken major positions in – and I trade around them. While I could have taken a handsome profit on these stocks, I have held onto them basically because I didn't feel there was alternative stock that I wanted to invest in. Of course, I could have sold and rebought. However this involves making an assumption that the stock will sink to levels that would return me a profit on repurchase – taking into account brokerage, stamp duty and tax costs. I'm not prepared to play the market game with my core portfolio and will remain invested provided I'm confident that the fundamentals remain sound.

The number of stocks you have depends on your financial position and objectives, but you might find it unwieldy if you go beyond a dozen. You should try and diversify over a number of sectors, but this need not happen all at once. It may take years to build a portfolio, and you never really stop. Often, when considering whether to buy a new stock, the yardstick you use is your existing stock, particularly if you don't want to put more money into the market. I swap my shares around, not based on what I originally paid for them, but on what I think the future holds for that particular stock and whether or not I can make more money in something else. This doesn't always work out, as you'll have noted from my disastrous sale of BHP to buy Transurban. Since BHP had been one of my core holdings, I should have been a lot more cautious and taken more advice before I sold. Before you take a major step, always get a second opinion.

Generally, most advisers would recommend that you start your portfolio with some blue-chip stocks: the banks, a resources stock, telecommunications, media and retail – and build on these. Sometimes cyclical stocks will be recommended. These are stocks that move in cycles, such as building stocks, which may be entering a recovery phase. Defensive stocks are those in companies that produce products that people are always going to want, for example food – not exciting, but pretty safe.

You're not always going to pick winners but, hopefully, the winners you pick will far outweigh the dogs.

A Portfolio that Grew from $2500 to $70,000

Some years ago, married friends of mine decided to start putting money into shares. The couple's financial resources were limited and they had no experience in the stockmarket. Their first purchase was 100 National Australia Bank shares each. (This gave them two opportunities to use the bank's share purchase plan.) They also signed up for the dividend reinvestment plan and the share purchase plan, and have increased their holdings every six months. At last count they had 1200 NAB each – and had only paid brokerage and stamp duty on their initial purchase.

Their next purchase was BHP, where again they've been reinvesting their dividends. After that they bought into the final tranche of the Commonwealth Bank, and both Telstra floats. They also bought 500 Coles Myer shares and later Woolworths shares. When they first bought NAB their 200 shares were about $11 per share, making a total investment of about $2500 (including brokerage). This is pretty modest by any standard.

Since then they have dripped money into the market, taking advantage of new floats and share reinvestment and purchase plans. During this time they bought, then sold, Amcor – after we'd decided that the money could be better invested elsewhere.

They got quite a shock when I pointed out that the current value of their portfolio was about $70,000. If I had initially suggested to them that they put this kind of money into shares they would have thought me certifiable. The only disagreement we had was over the purchase of the final tranche of CBA, when they shouted at me that I didn't seem to understand that they couldn't afford to buy, and I shouted back that they couldn't afford not to buy!

Hopefully, their next move will be to diversify further – possibly into the entertainment or media industries. You'll notice that all of their stocks are in well-established companies whose businesses they can understand.

It's worth noting that dividend reinvestment plans and share purchase plans can be cancelled by a company at any time. This usually happens when the share price has dropped considerably – and can cause you great frustration. On the other hand, think how much dilution the new shares issued under the plans would bring to an already struggling share price.

Steering Clear of Smokes and Battery Hens

Deciding what is or isn't ethical is up to you. I don't invest in cigarette companies, those that practise intensive livestock farming or other activities I consider unethical. This means that I wouldn't invest in Goodman Fielder with its hen batteries, Ridley Corporation with its piggeries or OAMPS for funding other companies' legal actions for a slice of the profit. On the other hand, I have no objection to alcohol or gaming stocks (as a breeder of racehorses, deploring the latter would be pretty hypocritical). But I strongly recommend that you don't base investment decisions (as distinct from lifestyle decisions) solely on the criterion that a company is doing something you approve of. *Never confuse investing for profit with lifestyle choices.* On the other hand, it's not a good idea to invest in something of which you strongly disapprove.

> #### POKIES POLLUTED A PORTFOLIO
> My cousin – who doesn't buy alcohol or gaming stocks – invested heavily in a company whose holdings included an environmental waste management group. This put him in the happy position of making money while supporting a virtuous activity. Unfortunately, the environmental waste project failed to get off the ground, and the company turned to manufacturing state-of-the-art poker-machine games. My cousin was mortified. Since then he has been in contact with the chairman of the holding company who has assured him the poker-machines were not envisaged as being a long-term, mainstream activity.

I believe you can take ethical investment to extremes. I know people who won't invest in the banks because they may be lending money for enterprises they disapprove of. Others disapprove of the fees and branch closures. However, since superannuation funds own bank shares, anyone who's in superannuation is in fact an owner of the bank whose profits they complain about. Personally, I'm banking on bank profits (bad pun) to provide for my retirement. However, I'd sell my bank shares immediately if there were signs of any return to the irresponsible lending practices of the eighties, which saw so many of our banks sail close to the wind. But this decision would be based on economic rather than moral grounds.

Occasionally, I put money into projects that sound sensible and appeal to me on a personal level, but I only invest money I can afford to lose in these speculative enterprises.

> ### TAKING A CALCULATED RISK...
> ### BY BACKING A RESEARCH PROJECT
> Because I'm interested in diet as a means of controlling menopause symptoms, I bought shares in Novogen, a company that produces Promensil, which is made from red clover. Although Novagen manufactures a product, its shares haven't returned a dividend, as all the earnings are ploughed back into research and promotion. I acquired these shares speculatively, before anything was actually produced. I won't be relying on them as a foundation for my future wealth, even though the share price has increased since purchase.

'When Should I Sell?'

You receive a call from your broker telling you a company is in trouble, and to get out immediately. The decision is easy: *sell*.

Thankfully, most of the time the issue is not as clear-cut as this. I believe there are two *major reasons* why you would consider selling particular shares:

1. **Because you think the share price is about to go down.** This could be for several reasons:
   - You think the general market is going to crash because, for example, interest rates look like going up or there is a frenzy of speculation.
   - You think the market is overheated and, for example, high-tech stocks, which are selling on unrealistic price earnings ratios, will fall and bring down the rest of the market.
   - You want to lock in profits on stocks you think might fall.
   - You've had a bad personal experience with a company – and have learned of other investors with similar complaints.
   - You think that the market or that particular stock is going to fall. For example, management appears to be losing the plot, perhaps racking up large amounts of debt for overpriced acquisitions or capital works. (BHP and Crown both did this.)
   - There are bad product reports, for example, faulty pacemakers.
   - You went to the annual general meeting and were unimpressed. (This happened to me at one company's annual general meeting a few years ago when there was not enough room for shareholders to get into the meeting. This showed a lack of foresight, organisation and planning which was being replicated in the way they ran the business.)
   - New information is published that shows the company is under-performing, the most blatant being a profit warning from the company itself.
   - There are problems in the whole sector. For example, the gold sector has declined due to the central bank's selling policies.
   - You think the price is going to slide, and you want to sell with the intention of buying back in at a cheaper price.

2. **You have better things to do with the money.**
   - You think your funds could be better employed elsewhere. This may be in a different stock, or out of the market altogether.

> **CUTTING MY LOSSES PAID OFF**
> Some years ago I felt Amcor was going nowhere, so I took a loss and swapped out of the stock into the ANZ bank. I believed I would make up the loss a lot more quickly in ANZ than by sticking with Amcor. This was one of the better decisions I've made. Amcor continued to slide while ANZ made significant gains.

- You need money for something else. My aunt, for example, sold shares when she needed money to buy a more expensive home.
- You still like the stock, but like something else even better.
- A rights options issue or placement is about to create a lot of new shares and you don't think the earnings will increase enough to counter the effects of dilution.

Other Reasons for Selling

- To realise a capital loss that will offset a capital gain. This sort of selling occurs a lot in June, so if you want a higher price you should act earlier than this.
- You wouldn't buy the stock if it were offered today, so why hang on to it.
- The share price has risen to the extent that it seriously unbalances your portfolio – that is, you have just too many eggs in that particular basket and need to diversify.

To Sum Up

In the final analysis, these decisions are up to you. We all have different needs and motivations. But the one thing we should have in common is that our reasons for selling or buying should be based on company and economic research and not on personal whim. *Buying and selling shares* is not like taking a lottery ticket or backing a horse. *It must always be regarded as an investment decision.*

10

RESEARCHING THE MARKET

As I've said before, it's vitally important that you research the companies whose shares you are buying. Recently, I was discussing this imperative in a class, when one of my students said she might have done the wrong thing. When I asked what she meant, she replied that she had bought shares in a mining company because she liked the name. Unhappily (despite the name!) they were performing very poorly. This took me back a bit. People back horses because they 'like the name', but this was the first time I had heard of anyone using this approach to buy shares. I am confident that Lizzie would have done better using this method to select horses rather than as a way to buy shares. The minimum bet on the TAB is 50 cents, considerably less than the minimum amount needed to invest in the sharemarket. The reason I mention this story is to try to convince you that, despite these being the days of the 'hot tip', investing in the sharemarket is not a lottery. It's like life – you usually get out what you put in. *Effort rather than money is the key to long-term success.*

'Where Do I Start?'

There are many ways you can research the stockmarket in general and individual stocks in particular. And, as I have already recommended, you shouldn't overlook your personal experiences.

Keep Clippings Folder

As a first step, I suggest you establish a separate folder for each stock you are interested in, placing in it relevant newspaper clippings, brokers' reports, magazine articles and any other printed information.

The Print Media

NEWSPAPERS

All major daily newspapers have a business section that provides information on the stockmarket. The *Australian Financial Review* is specifically targeted to investment matters and is particularly useful during company reporting seasons (February/March and July/August).

On Mondays the *Financial Review* has details of all dividends that have been declared and not paid. On Fridays (at the time of writing) there is also an interesting section, Under Scrutiny, which features companies that have received queries from the Stock Exchange on their share price, complemented by the company response and market rumours about the stock. See also page 138.

MAGAZINES

These include *Business Review Weekly*, *Shares*, *Personal Investment* and *Money*. All can provide useful background information and commentary, but should not be uncritically followed.

By the time the magazines are on the market, the information, particularly stock tips, is out of date. If a week is a long time in politics, 20 minutes is a long time on the sharemarket. The Stock Exchange provides prices and company announcements free of charge after a time-lapse of 20 minutes.

> ### Punter Doubles His Money – while 'Experts' Languish
>
> In a competition organised by the Melbourne *Age* in 1998, several brokers, a specialist magazine and a punter 'Lucky Phil' were each given $50,000 to see how they fared during the year. Because Phil was gambling on the horses he was limited to spending $1000 per week (in case he blew it in the first few months). Midway through the competition one of the brokers dropped out (he was doing very badly), while the rest of them staggered on with very poor results. The shining exception was Lucky Phil who, by the end of the year – and with the aid of a few great trifectas – had just about doubled his money!

Stockbrokers' Mailouts

The timing and quality of material available from stockbrokers varies considerably. Some brokers send out door-stopper-sized reports each quarter, while others are content with a very basic two-page mailout. But forget the *quantity*, if you track the advice you receive over a six-month period you'll get some idea of the *quality*. As with magazines and newspapers, brokers' research is likely to be well and truly out of date by the time you receive it.

Brokers are usually anxious not to offend large companies (it doesn't help their analysts obtain information), and may slant their research more favourably than can be strictly justified. Broker material will always contain 'buy' and 'sell' recommendations, *but under no circumstances should you invest merely on the basis of these written reports*. Always check back with the originating broker, and get a second opinion before following any advice sent out in the mail. Other terms that brokers use are 'hold, lighten and accumulate'. These terms are usually explained in the material they have sent you, but if you don't understand ring up and ask.

Again, keep in mind that brokers don't earn income if you hold the same stock forever. Nor of course do they retain your custom if their advice is poor. If you're on the mailing list of more than one broker see if there is any consensus among the various reports. On occasions brokers may be holding large sell orders for a stock, and therefore be biased toward you buying that stock. They may also try to push you into taking part in floats they are having difficulty filling. Always try to do some independent research.

NEWSLETTERS

There are several independent newsletters published. These include Huntley's *Your Money Weekly* and *Small Companies Guide*. *The Intelligent Investor* is another independent newsletter. Normally you can obtain free trial copies of these publications before subscribing. Mostly these are reports aimed at educating the investor rather than pushing any particular barrow. However, one independent newsletter appeared to be advising subscribers to buy a certain stock at the same time the proprietors were selling the stock. Again, don't act on recommendations without double-checking with other sources. Subscribers can also obtain Huntley's research on the Internet.

OTHER PUBLICATIONS

Several publications cover the top 500 or 100 companies. These are very useful reference tools, and are available at major bookstores or by ordering over the Internet. *Huntley's Top 500* is particularly useful if you're interested in researching a specific sector of the market, as all companies are cross-referenced by industry sector.

ANNUAL REPORTS

The best way of finding out about a company is by reading its annual report. Of course companies will seek to put the best possible spin on their activities for the year. Most reports emphasise what the company wants you to focus on, 'the good news', and downplay areas they aren't so thrilled about, 'the not-so-good news'. When all else fails they fill the report with inane pictures of happy staff/customers or, as a last resort, photographs of the premises. This in itself tells you something about the company's performance for the year!

Unfortunately for the spin doctors there are statutory reporting requirements that no amount of happy snaps can disguise. Look at *the five-year summary* to see how the company is really going. If the format has changed from the year before ask the company why. (It may be for clearer reporting or it may be to obscure inconvenient information.)

Oh Oh, happy snaps! I'll have to speak to my broker in the morning

In all company reports there is an opening section that tells you what the company does, which may sometimes surprise you. After that come the accounts, and the notes to the accounts. The notes are not an addendum, but are there to explain the accounts, so don't switch off but try to read and make sense of the figures. There is also a section setting out the number of shares held by the company directors (do they have faith in their product?) and a list of the top 20 shareholders (are these well-known institutions?).

If there is something you don't understand, contact the company and ask for an explanation. Usually a polite letter to the chairman will bring forth a considered and informative response.

> ### A Letter Cuts More Ice than a Phone Call
> My cousin and I both own shares in a small company, although his holding is much larger than mine. When he rang the company for clarification on some points he was politely fobbed off. But when I subsequently wrote to the chairman I received a pleasant and informative reply that satisfied all our queries.

Apart from the annual report there is also a six-monthly financial report to shareholders. Even if you're not a shareholder you can telephone a company and ask for an annual report. I've never had a company refuse to send one, though on one occasion a report that was promised failed to materialise. Again, that told me something about the company. I don't object to companies asking their shareholders to tick a box if they prefer not to receive a copy of the annual report. But I abhor the practice of some companies that reverse the onus, and ask you to tell them if you want one – usually not even including a self-addressed envelope. Clearly costs have overcome the desire to keep shareholders informed. Remember, as well, there is always the annual general meeting when you can question the directors personally about the company's performance.

The Internet

This has become the single greatest source of information available to stockmarket investors, and the information available is increasing daily.

Company Sites

Virtually all the major listed companies have websites, with varying quality of information. The best ones have descriptions of the company's activities, copies of annual reports, company announcements and transcripts of interviews given by the company's senior executives. They also have specific shareholder sections with the facility to e-mail the company with any further questions you may have. Other sites, such as Woolworths, are not only informative but rather fun – with recipes and shopping lists.

NEWSPAPERS

The *Australian Financial Review* (**www.afr.com.au**) has a comprehensive site which, for a fee, enables you to search archived material. Attached to this site is the Trading Room (**www.tradingroom.com.au**) where a wealth of information is available on individual stocks. There's a small charge for recent announcements and prices ('recent' is within 20 minutes). You can establish credit with the Trading Room either over the Net or by telephone. Each user has a password, and so far I've had no problem with security. The *AFR* is one of my favourite sites – where I live, copies of the paper are a long time arriving.

The *Age* (**www.theage.com.au**) has business news along with general content. Apart from the business section, there are many other features, like theatre and restaurant reviews.

The *Sydney Morning Herald* (**www.smh.com.au**) also has a business section and general content.

MAGAZINES

Selected stories from *Shares* (**www.sharesdaily.com.au**) and *Personal Investor* (**www.personalinvestor.com.au**) are published on the Net, and links are provided from these sites to other magazines such as *Business Review Weekly*. Some articles are also archived and can be accessed for a modest charge. The *Shares* site is updated daily, but is only available to magazine subscribers who pay an additional charge for the service.

THE AUSTRALIAN STOCK EXCHANGE

The Australian Stock Exchange (**www.asx.com.au**) has its own site. This site provides a wealth of information. You can find out about upcoming floats, access company announcements, and receive delayed share prices. It features educational material on how the stockmarket works, how to invest in shares, and managing your portfolio. There is an on-line link with a bookshop, and simulated sharemarket games you can play before investing.

There is also a comprehensive broker referral service and a grid containing the names of different on-line service providers. The latter need to be selected carefully as some service providers offer very expensive services. Some are cheap, and some of the names given turn out to be simply advertisements for stockbrokers. There's also a lot of statistical information and advice on lunchtime lectures and stock exchange courses. This is not a site I use very much, but it can be a good starting point for a new investor.

Stockbrokers

Most stockbrokers have some presence on the web, and the research and services provided are increasing as on-line trading gains in popularity. The quality of the sites varies enormously. Several provide research, but much of it is totally out of date.

An on-line broker such as Commonwealth Securities (**www.comsec.com.au**) provides a great deal of free information to clients on the bigger listed companies, together with live share quotes and market depth. While their telephone service is at times appalling, their Internet site is usually reliable, and it is worth registering as a client to gain access to their data banks.

The most comprehensive full-service broker site is that of Shaw Stockbroking (**www.cgoli.com.au**). This site has up-to-date research, a news and views section and a discussion forum, which is one of the few on the Net that tends to focus on major stocks. There is also an e-mail facility that informs you when new research becomes available.

Try **www.brokerchoice.com.au**, **www.directinfo.com.au** or **www.yourbroker.com.au** to compare details of the services offered by on-line brokers.

Most of the stockbroking sites have special access for clients, with varying levels of information.

Service Providers

A number of these can be accessed through the ASX site. I often use Investorweb (**www.investorweb.com.au**). This site has some free data and other user-pays information. There is also a series of forums, some which are free, and a premium forum that you pay for.

Stockwatch (**stockwatch.com.au**) has live share prices and other information. This service is free if you use Internet service-providers OzEmail, Voyager Access One or Camtech, with a monthly subscription fee payable by everyone else. Weblink (**www.weblink.com.au**) provides prices and other data for a fee. Hotcopper (**hotcopper.com.au**) is mainly dedicated to forums which are essentially user chat rooms.

Chat Groups and Forums

These mostly contain comments on speculative stocks, some of which are made by highly enthusiastic or desperate users (depending on your viewpoint). Obviously you must be extremely careful about taking notice of any tips on these sites. Even though careful guidelines are spelt out on what can and can't be said in a forum, the stocks discussed are frequently obscure and the motives of the people raising them are unknown. Personally, I place very little credence on these and only log on out of curiosity or for educational research reasons – that is, I trawl through them so I can tell my classes what's in them. It's usually a lot of drivel!

The Australian Securities and Investments Commission (ASIC)

The ASIC (**www.asic.gov.au**) site explains about investing, and points out the traps for the unwary. It offers excellent general advice, and you can find out whether a particular company exists or whether your financial adviser is still licensed to practise. You can also do company searches and many other useful things.

The Australian Tax Office

The ATO (**www.ato.gov.au**) has an extremely comprehensive site where you can access extensive information on tax matters including tax rulings, draft determinations and judicial decisions.

Search Engines

You can use Yahoo or any of the other search engines to find any site whose address is not known. Just type in the company name and, if it has a site it will be thrown up. Just click on to the site and the search engine will take you there. Any sites that you frequently use should be bookmarked for easy future reference.

Broadcasting Services

Television

Business Sunday (on Channel Nine at 8 am Sundays) is a quality program that looks at the week's events and has interviews with senior managers of companies. A market wrap organised by the *Australian Financial Review* is screened at 8 pm weeknights on the CNBC station of all pay TV services.

Channel 28 screens a business review program from the United States at 12 noon from Tuesday to Saturday, and any television set with a Teletext service provides free 20-minute delayed sharemarket quotes, from 10.20 am to 7 pm.

Radio

ABC radio in every Australian state broadcasts stockmarket reports. Check times in your local media guide. In my home town (Melbourne) ABC Radio 3LO 774 has a market cross with a stockmarket report at 9.30 am and 5.30 pm each weekday. This station also has an excellent finance section at 10 am on Mondays (when Gavin Ross answers listeners' questions) as well as a finance segment at 8.30 am on Saturdays. In Victoria, Investorweb and others sponsor a radio program, *Dollars at Work*, on Sunday mornings from 9 am to 10 am on an AM band, 3RPH 1179, and on various other country FM stations including Bay FM.

Never blindly accept the advice given out on radio programs. With the exception of Gavin Ross (whom I consider the best of the experts) some stations have at times given out questionable advice, particularly in the area of taxation. Any comments broadcasters make are meant to be general guides, and may not be applicable to your situation.

Reading the Sharemarket Prices in Newspapers

I'm often asked what the headings mean on the price reporting section of the newspapers. The following guide does not include all the factors that may be listed, but is a summary of the terms used in the *Australian Financial Review*. The terms appear listed from left to right:

52 Week High/Low The highest and lowest sales price the share has reached during the past 52 weeks of trading on the ASX – that is, how the share price has performed during the past 12 months.

Day's High/Low: The highest and lowest price recorded during the trading day. This gives you an indication of how much a stock price fluctuates within a day.

ASX Code The three-letter code given to all stock for identification purposes – for example, Woolworths is WOW. You will need this code to look up information on the Internet.

Company Name Self-explanatory.

Market Call Code The numbers you need if you want to use the market call telephone system to check a share price.

Last Sale The final sale price recorded at the close of business on the previous day. This is the figure used to value a share portfolio at any particular time.

+ or - The movement of a share price over that of the previous day.

Vol. 100s The total volume (in hundreds) of shares traded that day.

Quote Buy The highest price the buyer (bidder) was prepared to pay for the shares.

Quote Sell The lowest price the seller (offerer) was prepared to sell the shares for.

Dividend c Per Share The last annual dividend paid by the company.

Dividend Times Cov The number of times the dividend per share is covered by the earnings per share (EPS). (Dividends are paid from the earnings of a company.) This is expressed as a percentage and is calculated by dividing the EPS by the DPS and multiplied by 100.

NTA Net Asset Backing is the *tangible* asset backing per share (excludes items like goodwill). This is calculated by dividing the net tangible assets by the number of shares on issue.

Div Yield % This is the amount of income a share is yielding. It is calculated by dividing the current dividend per share by the last sale price and multiplying by 100. It doesn't include franking credits and, because the dividend is historic, doesn't provide an accurate guide to future yield. If the dividend remains static and the share price goes up, the yield will automatically go down and vice versa.

Earn. Share c Earnings per share (in cents) is the company's net profit divided by the number of shares on issue. Again, the earnings are historic and don't represent future earnings.

P/E Ratio This is the current share price divided by the earnings per share. This is one of the fundamental ratios and has been examined in depth in Chapter 8. Remember, the share price is current but the earnings are historic.

Don't Forget to Keep Records!

Not only do you need to know how your share portfolio is performing, but the Australian Taxation Office has an interest in it as well. For taxation purposes you need to keep a record of all investment income received during the fiscal year, together with any expenses involved in earning that income. Keep these records in a safe place for at least five years after you have lodged your tax return. In the case of shares, the major documents you need to retain are:

- Your contract notes (the ones from the stockbroker referred to in Chapter 3).
- Your statement of holdings received from the company (either through CHESS or from the share registry).
- Your dividend statements.

For easy reference you need to keep a register of your transactions. This can be done manually or with a computer spreadsheet. Whatever way you choose you will need two separate parts to the register. One part must contain details of the *income* you have received from the shares. The other part must contain details of *the date you acquired the share and capital cost of the shares*.

It's particularly important you maintain this 'capital' register if you are buying and selling shares regularly, or if you are participating in dividend reinvestment or share purchase plans. The register need not be elaborate but it must be accurate and up to date. It's easiest if you discipline yourself to enter the file details as soon as you receive them. While you can't claim brokerage and stamp duty as a tax deduction, they do form part of the capital base of the share (Chapter 4). However there are other deductions that can be claimed – such as magazine subscriptions. Once again, these should be written down and all receipts kept.

Any computerised records you keep must be in a form that Tax Office staff can access and understand. Remember, in taxation matters the onus is on you to prove your claims, not on the Tax Department to disprove them – a very significant reversal of the innocent till proven guilty rule applicable in the criminal justice system!

FREQUENTLY (AND NOT-SO-FREQUENTLY) ASKED QUESTIONS

Some of the questions I'm often asked during my classes haven't been included in the main text of this book. I can't cover them all, but have listed some here – along with my answers.

Q *What is an institution?*

A In stockmarket parlance an 'institution' means an institutional investor. These are large funds (e.g. superannuation funds, managed funds, insurance companies and banks) that invest the collective money of other investors. These are the investors whose buying and selling move the market, and whose votes really count if push comes to shove. Management changes at both Coles Myer and BHP were largely the result of pressure from institutional shareholders.

Q *What is an analyst?*

A An analyst is employed by a broking firm or institution to research the future prospects of companies. This research includes looking at the general economic climate and the likely prospects for the industry sector which the company is involved in. Analysts usually use computer modelling and onsite company visits. Failing that, they are adept with crystal balls and tarot cards!

The opinion of a prominent analyst, particularly in the United States, can have a major influence on the institution or company they work for – and even on the market in general. Analysts who give unfavourable reports on a company aren't likely to be welcomed back by that company. And if the analyst works for a broking firm a nasty report can sour relations with the broker as well. Even scrupulously fair analysts are never right all the time and spend a lot of their time revising their forecasts in the light of unexpected circumstances (so they loathe uncertainty).

Q *What is an abnormal (or an unusual)?*

A An item is classified as 'an abnormal' in the profit and loss statement of a company when an event occurs in the normal business dealings of the company, but is not likely to be repeated. For example, an abnormal profit may be declared because the bank has sold a building, or an abnormal loss because a company has 'written down' assets in value. These events should be discounted if you're looking at the ongoing performance of the company, because they only have a one-off impact on company earnings.

Q *Who is 'Mr Market'?*

A A mythical person who represents the collective mood of the market. On the day Kuwait was invaded, Mr Market got very depressed and saw nothing but gloom and doom for the sharemarket. After Baghdad was bombed he cheered up considerably and bounced back. Mr Market doesn't care about the intrinsic value of companies but is preoccupied with emotions. He was maniacally optimistic about the future of all high-tech companies until a legal judgement went against Microsoft. This made him very pessimistic and resulted in the 'tech wreck'. As I write, he is very excited about the biotechnology stocks.

FREQUENTLY (AND NOT-SO-FREQUENTLY) ASKED QUESTIONS

Q What are day traders?

A Would-be masters of the universe who have given up their day jobs, bought an expensive piece of computer equipment and trade frequently in an attempt to make a profit. This was easy before the tech wreck but is more challenging in a falling market. They frequently appear in chat rooms and forums boasting of their successes, trying to talk a stock up and getting nasty with anyone presumptuous enough to disagree with them. Generally they appear in these forums under pseudonyms like Rambo, Darth Vader, Dominator, Savvy, etc.

Q What is ramping?

A Promoting a share price by the use of either true or false information, so that the shares can be sold for a profit. This is a general tactic employed by day traders in chat rooms and forums (which is why they get so nasty when someone disagrees with them).

Q What is spamming?

A Sending the same message many times to numerous chat rooms and forums in the hope that if you say something often enough someone will believe it – and act on it. This action is of course designed to benefit the person doing the spamming.

Q What is a dead cat bounce?

A If you throw a dead cat from the top of a very tall building it allegedly bounces when it hits the ground. In the stockmarket it represents a major fall in share prices followed by a small bounce back – after which the market returns to a comatose position.

Q *What is a suckers' rally?*

A This is a bigger rebound than a dead cat bounce — designed to trick the gullible into thinking a new market boom is underway. The 'suckers' move in and the market then falls down again.

Q *What is insider trading?*

A Illegal share-trading on the basis of price-sensitive information unavailable to the public at large (but available to company 'insiders'). ASIC and the ASX make valiant attempts to stop this practice, but to date they have had little success.

Q *What is a thin market?*

A This is when very low volumes of shares are traded. In such a market, any large trade has a bigger impact on the market than it would when volumes are high.

Q *What is a Chinese Wall?*

A An imaginary wall between one section of a business and another, so that employees in one part of a firm are theoretically unaware of what employees in another part of the firm are doing. This is supposed to stop conflict of interest. For example, you might find employees in one part of the firm trading shares in a company that other employees in another part of the same firm are looking at in preparation for a takeover offer being made. Personally, I think illusions should be left to stage performances... but then I'm not known for my imagination.

Q *What is an underwriter to a float?*

A This is the broker or bank that not only arranges a float but agrees to take up any shares that are not sold. Clearly there is a conflict of interest between the vendors of a company, who want the best possible price for their company, and the underwriters who want to underwrite it at the most saleable price. Melbourne IT was a good example of what can happen in this situation. The broker insisted that $2.20 was the best possible share price for the company, and the top value they would underwrite at. The day the company floated, the shares closed above $8. A nice profit for anyone allocated shares by the broker.

Q *What is churning?*

A Turning shares over so frequently that it enriches the broker and impoverishes you. On-line brokers really love the day traders! Win or lose, the brokers collect the commission.

Q *Can you go broke taking a profit?*

A Yes, if you sell your good stocks when they have achieved modest gains in price and hang on to your losers, hoping they'll come good ('watering the weeds').

Q *What is window dressing?*

A A practice often engaged in by fund managers at the end of the financial year. It involves pushing up the price of stock (usually widely held shares) to improve portfolio returns the day the books close.

Q *What is an independent valuation?*

A When a company receives a takeover offer the directors of the target company are obliged to give their opinion on whether or not shareholders should accept the offer. To substantiate their opinion they engage an 'independent' expert to value the company. This can present a few problems. Firstly, no matter how independent the experts are, they are being paid by the company. Secondly, if the company is taken over the directors will usually lose their jobs. This means that if they are large shareholders in the company you can expect them to be more shareholder-oriented than if they are merely paid to sit on the board. In this situation beware of the advice of those whose interests do not coincide with your own.

Q *What is a speculator?*

A The same as a gambler who is prepared to stake money on a chance for hopefully high rewards. Losing the lot does not perturb them.

Q *What is a dog?*

A A very bad stock. (A bad racehorse, on the other hand, is called a cat).

Q *What does it mean when the market tanks?*

A A general collapse has taken place.

AFTERWORD

In the Introduction I emphasised that understanding how the sharemarket operates requires a fair bit of effort, and that you may feel discouraged at times. As you'll now know, I've made more than my fair share of financial mistakes over the years. I hope you're able to learn from these without having to experience them yourself. However, it's unrealistic to imagine you'll never make a mistake. I must admit that revisiting the past in this book has sometimes been painful for me. But rather than dwelling on my failures, I try to take a deep breath, analyse what went wrong, learn and move on. Should you make any financial blunders of your own, I suggest you try to do the same thing.

No doubt you've found some chapters more difficult than others, but don't worry if you haven't understood everything. It's all a matter of consciousness-raising and learning to focus on the subject. It will help if you make a point of watching and listening to TV and radio finance programs (see Chapter 10). You may have to force yourself to do this at first, or perhaps you can gently slide into it. My cousin sometimes buys a small number of shares of a company he's interested in to help him properly focus his attention on the company. As I've already said, money is interesting, especially your own! One of my over-fifty friends, who is new to the market, is now a fascinated watcher of CNBC on cable TV, and is preparing to buy a computer so she can launch herself onto the market.

Looking back, I realise that while financial independence was a priority for me, achieving it did not begin in the cradle. In my twenties, despite having a series of well-paid jobs, I spent most of my income on travel and clothes. A day came when, sitting on the beach with my cousin, he asked me incredulously, 'You mean you haven't got anything?' I had to admit that apart from my education and skills this was true. In fact, at that time a family bereavement had plunged me into debt. My cousin and I had a little talk, and I went off and had a bit of a think. After that I started saving, bought an investment property (with borrowed money), sold it and bought a home. I also began to save through the superannuation system (which was vastly different in those days and gave me access to my funds when I left employment).

Had I been smarter, I would also have learned about, and become active in, the sharemarket much earlier. However, this early preparation proved useful as it made changing direction twenty years later much easier. But, of course, that was not planned. At twenty-seven, I never dreamed I could be unemployable at fifty. In fact, I never imagined that I would ever turn fifty!

I suspect that most young people feel the same way. Superannuation, shares and enforced retirement are the last thing that most 'twenty-somethings' think about. But, ideally, this is the time to begin some kind of long-term financial plan. But don't lose heart if you're much, much older. It's never too late to take control of your finances. You may be more comfortable setting yourself formal goals with specific targets you can achieve along the way. If you take this approach, try to gradually extend yourself beyond your comfort zone.

Some of your goals may be difficult to achieve, and you're sure to run into obstacles along the way. But overall you should find pleasure in what you are and what you do. To keep your finances in order, you must have your life in order.

I worked for many years in a job that was unsatisfying and, in the end, soul-destroying. Despite having some prestige and being well paid I was very unhappy. This unhappiness translated to inertia, and it was very difficult to change my life. I remember discussing this with my aunt — and lamenting the fact that I'd spent years and years working at a job I didn't enjoy, because it was the safe option. Was this to be my life?

I now realise I was saved by my retrenchment — disastrous as it seemed at the time. Life for me *did* start (or restart) at fifty. After surviving the shellshock, I was determined to make a better fist of it than I had done before. Fortunately I didn't take the status of the job seriously; I was not the job. It didn't worry me that a lot of 'friends' no longer wanted to know me, and in some cases seemed to take pleasure in my being unemployed.

Personal calamity is a good way of finding out who your true friends are.

If, like me, you are starting over, you must be prepared to take advantage of any opportunities that are presented to you, however small — not simply for where they might lead, but because you learn from them and want to do them well.

I did my Master's degree for myself, not to enhance any future job prospects. I then got serious about the sharemarket and enjoyed researching companies. I started teaching because I was passionate about the subject matter and found I enjoyed tutoring adult women. Over the years I have had many good experiences flow from these classes, and have met some truly wonderful women. The day that teaching becomes a chore, I will give it up.

When I left work my friends fell into two distinct categories: those who thought my life had come to an end, and those who felt I had the life skills to forge a new and satisfying future. I don't want to choose your friends, but being around people whose anxieties reinforce your own is not a good idea. Even when I was feeling good, an hour with a friend who was worried about my future 'now I was on the corporate scrap-heap' would send me into a fit of self-doubt and despair.

I have a friend who reserves her pessimism for her own situation, but is neutral about mine. The last time I saw her, she was resigned to losing all the money she had invested in Telstra, on the basis that she 'supposed it didn't matter anyway'. I tried to reassure her that though the share price may have slumped the total collapse of one of our largest and most profitable companies was highly improbable. But I doubt if it changed her opinion that her investment was doomed. It's the way she views the world. *If you feel fragile, keep company with your more positive and balanced friends — people who are supportive and push you along.* At the same time, try not to drag them down with constant repetition of your problems.

There are many people who have given me great support and encouragement in the last ten years and I am profoundly grateful to them. Part of the yogic experience is leaving your shoes and your problems at the door and focusing on your inner self. You will find that other people respect you when you respect yourself. One of the most dangerous myths is contained in the lyrics of a song dating back to the forties, and revived by Dean Martin in the fifties: 'You're No One Till Somebody Loves You'. What rubbish! Yet this is the attitude earlier generations of women grew up with.

Finally, inaction is possibly your greatest enemy. 'If your ship has not come in, swim out to it'. Start doing some research, start asking questions and don't get discouraged if you make a mistake. If things go wrong, go for a long walk to regain your equilibrium. It's never too early or too late to educate yourself — and if you've read this book, or even skimmed through it, you have just taken a positive first step.

Congratulations!

INDEX

'abnormals', 142
active funds, 65
acquisition of assets, 56
allocated pensions, 72
American Market, 50
All Ordinaries Index
   (All Ords), 47
All Ordinaries Accumulation
   Index, 49
analyst, 141
Australian Securities and
   Investment Commission
   (ASIC), 47
averaging down, 116
averaging up, 116

basic terms, 32
bonus shares, 36
borrowing to buy shares, 107
broadcasting services, 137
broker sponsorship, 44
brokers,
   choosing, 77
   how to find, 79
bear market, 41
bull market, 41

Capital Gains Tax (CGT), 56
Chinese Wall, 144
churning, 145
Coles Myer discount, 104
collectables, 24
company options, 45
contract notes, 43
convertible notes, 34
convertible preference shares, 34
converting preference shares, 33
cum dividend shares, 46

day traders, 143
dead cat bounce, 143
debt-to-equity ratio, 118
dilution, 35,

discount brokers, 75
disposal of assets, 56
dividend imputation, 52,
dividend payments, 46
dividend reinvestment plans
   (DRPs), 30
dividend yield, 101
dot coms, 91
'dripping', 116

earnings, 103
earnings per share, 35
ethical sharebuying, 124
ex-dividend shares, 45

fees and charges, 69
financial advisers, 70
franking credit, 53
franked dividends, 55
full-service brokers, 75
fundamental analysis, 120

Goods and Services Tax
   (GST), 62
growth investments, 17
growth stocks, 104

income stocks, 104
independent valuation, 146
index or passive funds, 67
industrial shares, 88
inflation, 88
information on shares
   Internet, 133
   print media, 129
   radio, 137
   television, 137
insider trading, 144
instalment receipts, 32
instalment warrants, 109
institutions, 141
Internet information, 133
keeping records, 140

listing on the stockmarket, 25
managed funds, 63
margin call, 108

margin lending account, 108
market capitalisation, 34
Medicare levy, 54
Mr Market, 142

net tangible assets, 119
newspaper sharemarket prices, 138
non-growth investments, 17

ordinary shares, 32
overseas funds, 69

passive funds, 67
payout ratio, 103
placements, 38
portfolio size, 121
preference shares, 33
price earnings ratio (PER), 95
primary market, 28
print media information, 129
prospectus, 26

ramping, 143
record of investments, 140
real estate, 20
researching the market, 128

rights issues, 37
resource shares, 92
retirement products, 71
return on equity, 111
risk, 106

secondary market, 29
self-assessment, 51,
selling shares, 125
share buy-backs, 39
share splits, 35
share top-up plans, 30
shareholder discount schemes, 30
spamming, 143
speculators, 146
stags, 29
starting a portfolio, 110
Stock Exchange Automated Trading System (SEATS), 40
suckers' rally, 144
superannuation, 93

takeovers, 57
technical analysis, 120
thin market, 144
transaction brokers, 75

underwriters to a float, 145

when to sell, 125
window dressing, 145

Author's Note

Every effort has been made to ensure that this publication is free from error and/or omission as at the date of printing, but neither the publisher nor the author can be held responsible for any information tendered, or for subsequent changes to taxation (or other) legislation.

It must be emphasised that the material contained in this book is of the nature of general comment and does not constitute the giving of advice. Readers should not act on the basis of views expressed in this book without seeking professional advice with regard to their own circumstances.

The author and the publisher take no responsibility for any loss occasioned to any person or organisation (whether a purchaser of this publication or not) who acts or refrains from acting as a result of the information or views contained in this publication. The author may hold shares in any of the companies named in this publication, but this should not be construed as a recommendation to buy or to sell such shares.